# GOD'S PASSIONATE DESIRE

## Other Books by
## William A. Barry, SJ

*Contemplatives in Action: The Jesuit Way*
(with Robert G. Doherty)

*Finding God in All Things: A Companion to the Spiritual Exercises of
St. Ignatius*

*A Friendship Like No Other: Experiencing God's Amazing Embrace*

*God and You: Prayer as a Personal Relationship*

*A Hunger for God: Ten Approaches to Prayer*

*Letting God Come Close: An Approach to the Ignatian Spiritual
Exercises*

*Now Choose Life: Conversion as the Way to Life*

*Our Way of Proceeding: To Make the Constitutions of the Society of
Jesus and Their Complementary Norms Our Own*

*Paying Attention to God: Discernment in Prayer*

*The Practice of Spiritual Direction*
(with William J. Connolly)

*Seek My Face: Prayer as Personal Relationship in Scripture*

*Spiritual Direction and the Encounter with God:
A Theological Inquiry*

*What Do I Want in Prayer?*

*Who Do You Say I Am? Meeting the Historical Jesus in Prayer*

*With an Everlasting Love:
Developing an Intimate Relationship with God*

# GOD'S PASSIONATE DESIRE

WILLIAM A. BARRY, SJ

LOYOLAPRESS.
A JESUIT MINISTRY
Chicago

# LOYOLA PRESS.
## A JESUIT MINISTRY

3441 N. Ashland Avenue
Chicago, Illinois 60657
(800) 621-1008
www.loyolapress.com

This is a revised edition of *God's Passionate Desire: And Our Response* originally published in 1993 by Ave Maria Press, Notre Dame, Indiana.

Unless otherwise noted, Scripture quotations contained herein are from the New Revised Standard Version Bible: Catholic Edition, copyright © 1993 and 1989 by the Division of Christian Education of the National Council of the Churches of Christ in the U.S.A. Used by permission. All rights reserved.

The quotations from *The Spiritual Exercises* are taken from Louis J. Puhl, trans., *The Spiritual Exercises of St. Ignatius: Based on Studies in the Language of the Autograph* (Chicago: Loyola Press, 1968). Used with permission.

"Scaffolding" (pp. 3–4) and "Storm on an Island" (p. 52) by Seamus Heaney are from *Death of a Naturalist* (London: Faber and Faber, 1969). Used with permission of Faber and Faber and Farrar, Straus and Giroux, LLC.

The diary entries by Etty Hillesum (pp. 29, 41, 76–85) are from *An Interrupted Life: The Diaries, 1941–1943, and Letters from Westerbork*, trans. Arnold J. Pomerans (New York: Henry Holt, 1996). Used with permission of Henry Holt.

"The Story" (pp. 109–11) by Brendan Kennelly is from *A Time for Voices: Selected Poems, 1960–1990* (Newcastle upon Tyne, England: Bloodaxe Books, 1990). Used with permission of Bloodaxe Books.

The psalm by John Tully Carmody (p. 128) is from *God Is No Illusion: Meditations on the End of Life* (Valley Forge, PA: Trinity Press International, 1997), 126. Used with permission of Denise Lardner Carmody.

Chapters 1 and 12 first appeared in *America*. Chapters 2, 4, 7, and 10 first appeared in the *Tablet*. Chapters 6, 11, and 14 first appeared in *Human Development*. Permission to reprint is gratefully acknowledged.

*Cover design by Beth Herman*
*Interior design by Maggie Hong*

**Library of Congress Cataloging-in-Publication Data**
Barry, William A.
  God's passionate desire / William A. Barry.
     p. cm.
  Includes bibliographical references.
  ISBN-13: 978-0-8294-2703-5
  ISBN-10: 0-8294-2703-1
  1. Meditations. I. Title.
  BX2182.3.B37 2008
  242—dc22

                                        2007042167

Printed in the United States of America
      10 11 12 13 14 Versa 10 9 8 7 6 5 4 3 2

*To my dear friends*
John T. Carmody (d. 1995)
*and* Denise Lardner Carmody,
*lovers of and witnesses to*
*the mystery we call God*

And thou like adamant
draw mine iron heart.

John Donne

# CONTENTS

# ACKNOWLEDGMENTS

Many people have helped me put together these meditations. Those who confided in me their experiences of God and of resistance to God go unnamed, but they know how integral to this book they are and how grateful I am. I want to say a special thanks to my spiritual director, Anne Harvey, SND, who with great patience and insight helped me see where I was resisting the pull of my own deepest desire. Once again, I express my gratitude to my father and sisters for their fidelity to reading my writing and commenting favorably on it, and to Marika Geoghegan, my dear friend, who reads both critically and encouragingly.

During the writing of most of this book, I was provincial of the Jesuits of the New England Province. That I was able to write at all during that year is due to the quality of the Jesuits of my province, who made it relatively easy to be provincial, and especially to the staff who worked with me at the provincial office, all of whom made it a pleasure to enter the office and made my job easier and even enjoyable. And I am grateful to Frank Cunningham and the editorial staff of Ave Maria Press, the first publisher of this book, who helped me make my work more accessible to others.

I am deeply grateful to Joseph Durepos and the editors of Loyola Press for their desire to reprint this book as a companion to *A Friendship Like No Other*. The two books do complement and reinforce each other. So my gratitude to Loyola Press is doubled this year.

I have a strong attachment to *God's Passionate Desire* not only because of its content, about which I care deeply, but also because of its dedicatees, John and Denise Carmody. John and Denise authored many books separately and together about world religions and spirituality. They cared and care passionately about God and the things of God. John contracted multiple myeloma before the publication of this book and died two years after its publication, on September 23, 1995. He is now at home with God, whom he loved so much, and lives on in his books and in the hearts of Denise and those who continue to cherish his friendship and wisdom. After John's death, Denise published a collection of letters and psalms he wrote during his final illness. I have included one of the psalms as a fitting afterword to this second edition.

Of course, my deepest debt of gratitude is to God, who gives me the ability to write at all and the privilege to write about the most important relationship any of us will ever have. *Laus Deo semper.*

For this edition, I have made a number of stylistic changes and some changes to its content. May it continue to help people discover God's passionate love for them, and theirs for God.

# INTRODUCTION

If you are familiar with my writing on prayer, you know that I am fascinated by the deep desire planted in each of us for union with God, and, in connection with that, union with one another. At the same time, I continually note in myself and in those who have confided in me a strong resistance to the fulfillment of that desire—a fulfillment I believe is passionately desired by God. If you have this book in your hands, you already know something of what I mean. Like me, you want a closer relationship with God yet find yourself resisting God's advances.

I wrote this book for readers like you. It is a collection of meditations that I hope will help you not only make sense of the seeming paradox of wanting something so much and yet resisting its fulfillment, but also move toward your heart's desire.

The book has three parts. In the first, we will explore God's desire for a relationship of intimacy with each one of us and how we experience that desire. Here I hope to guide you toward recognizing your own foundational experiences of God and some of the consequences of taking those experiences seriously.

The second part looks at a few of the paradoxes entailed in this relationship. How do fear of God and attraction to God coexist? How can we trust a God who does not save us from awful sufferings? These are some of the questions I have had to face in my relationship with God, and in talking with others, I have found that I am not alone. I hope the meditations in this part will intrigue you and assist you in your own conversations with God.

The third part of the book focuses on the implications for our lives of friendship with God. In creating this world and us, God needs friends who will cooperate in the project Jesus called the kingdom. Here I hope to help you enter the conversation with God about your part in this project.

I dearly hope that you will find this book helpful to your developing relationship with God. As we begin, let us pray together these words of St. Anselm of Canterbury:

> Teach me to seek you,
> and reveal yourself to me as I seek;
> for unless you instruct me
> I cannot seek you,
> and unless you reveal yourself
> I cannot find you.
> Let me seek you in desiring you;
> let me desire you in seeking you.
> Let me find you in loving you;
> let me love you in finding you.

Part 1

# FOUNDATIONS

# Building a Relationship with God

In his poem "Scaffolding," Seamus Heaney uses the metaphor of scaffolding to say something profound about his relationship with a loved one. The couple in the poem have built the wall of their love so solidly that they do not need the scaffolding anymore.

> Masons, when they start upon a building,
> Are careful to test out the scaffolding;
>
> Make sure that planks won't slip at busy points,
> Secure all ladders, tighten bolted joints.
>
> And yet all this comes down when the job's done
> Showing off walls of sure and solid stone.

> So if, my dear, there sometimes seem to be
> Old bridges breaking between you and me
>
> Never fear. We may let the scaffolds fall
> Confident that we have built our wall.

I want to develop the metaphor in Heaney's poem so that we can see its application in the relationship God desires with us. Can we apply what we know of human relationships to our relationship with God?

## THE IMPORTANCE OF RITES IN HUMAN FRIENDSHIP

First, let's look at the development of a strong friendship between two human beings. What might be the scaffolding necessary for it? I am reminded of the fox who asked Antoine de Saint-Exupéry's little prince to become his friend. The little prince wants to know how to go about it, and the fox replies:

> You must be very patient. First you will sit down at a little distance from me—like that—in the grass. I shall look at you out of the corner of my eye, and you will say nothing . . . but you will sit a little closer to me, every day.

The next day when the prince comes, the fox tells him:

> It would have been better to come back at the same
> hour. If you come at just any time, I shall never know
> at what hour my heart is to be ready to greet you. . . .
> One must observe the proper rites.

The French of the last line is more concise: *Il faut des rites*; rites
are necessary.

Earlier in the conversation, the fox says:

> One only understands the things that one tames
> [befriends]. Men have no more time to understand any-
> thing. They buy things all ready made at the shops. But
> there is no shop anywhere where one can buy friend-
> ship, and so men have no friends any more.

In these days of instant friendship, such attention to rites may
seem arcane and a bit romantic. Television and film seem to
require little more for love between a man and a woman than
a passionate look before they are in bed together. The fact that
commitment in marriage or friendship seems more the exception than the norm may reveal the bankruptcy of the culture of
instant relationships. Perhaps Saint-Exupéry is not so romantic after all. Perhaps rites *are* necessary for developing a strong
friendship.

Joseph Flanagan, SJ, a professor of philosophy at Boston
College, has noted that Americans have lost the rites of courting
and dating. When those of us who are over fifty were growing

up, we had a pretty good idea of how to act with the opposite sex. It was a somewhat daunting prospect to begin the process of developing a relationship, but we knew the rites, as it were. Now many young people are at sea because there are few guidelines, few accepted ways of acting that allow for a gradual development of intimacy. As a result, young students heading off to college are barraged with courses and talks about the use of alcohol and drugs, date rape, and racial and sexual stereotyping. But most of the input is information. What seems terribly lacking are generally accepted rites of passage and standards of moral behavior that can guide young people as they explore new relationships and learn the ways of intimacy and friendship. Getting close to and befriending another person takes time and requires rites. We need to reestablish these rites, because they are the scaffolding that enables two people to build the wall of a sound and lasting friendship.

What are these rites? First, having felt an attraction to you, I try to spend time with you, perhaps at first seemingly by accident, in an attempt to get to know you better. As it becomes apparent that the attraction is mutual, we will make time to be with each other, to do things together. Then we will gradually reveal things about ourselves to each other. Finally, when both of us are relatively sure of the depth of our friendship, we will formalize what has become a reality. We will begin to date, or we will affirm that we are best friends, or we will in some other way acknowledge that we are special to each other. In the process of building our wall, we may have some difficult times, times when we fail to communicate, when we quarrel, when one or the other of us feels unappreciated. We are, after all, human beings, with all the foibles and fears we are heir to. We may each be as skittish as the fox in *The Little Prince*. But once we have befriended each other and established ties, then "we may let the scaffolds fall / Confident that we have built our wall."

## THE SCAFFOLDING NECESSARY FOR A FRIENDSHIP WITH GOD

Now let's see what might follow in our relationship with God. The analogy limps on the side of God but holds up quite well as far as we are concerned. We know from revelation that we exist because God desires us into being and keeps us in being. God, it would seem, is madly in love with us and is always attracted to us. The problem is that most of us do not really believe it. Many of us harbor an image of God as a taskmaster or even a tyrant because of psychological trauma or poorly assimilated teaching about God. As a result, the desire for God that is implanted deep in our hearts by creation is often muted, if not smothered, by fear of God. We need experiences of God as attractive. We have to give God a chance to prove to us that he really is our heart's love and desire.

As C. S. Lewis noted in his autobiography, *Surprised by Joy*, every so often we are overcome by a feeling of enormous well-being and a desire for "we know not what." This desire is what he calls joy, and he describes it as more satisfying than the fulfillment of any other desire, even though we recognize that it cannot be fully satisfied this side of heaven. We need to recall and savor these experiences of joy so that we will want to develop an intimate relationship of friendship and love with God. I have come to believe that these are experiences of our own creation. Moreover, I believe that they are the experiences that led St. Ignatius of Loyola to formulate his First Principle and Foundation at the beginning of *The Spiritual Exercises*. In this rather abstract statement, Ignatius shows that God creates each human being for union with the triune God, and that nothing but such union will ultimately satisfy us.

Here is an example of the welling up of such a desire in an ordinary experience, one that any teenager might have. In his memoir *Sacred Journey*, Frederick Buechner tells of an incident in Bermuda, where his mother had taken him and his brother after his father's suicide. Near the end of his stay, Buechner, then thirteen, was sitting on a wall with a girl who was also thirteen, watching ferries come and go. He recalls:

> Our bare knees happened to touch for a moment, and in that moment I was filled with such a sweet panic and anguish of longing for I had no idea what that I knew my life could never be complete until I found it. . . . It was the upward-reaching and fathomlessly hungering, heart-breaking love for the beauty of the world at its most beautiful, and, beyond that, for that beauty east of the sun and west of the moon which is past the reach

of all but our most desperate desiring and is finally the beauty of Beauty itself, of Being itself and what lies at the heart of Being.

Buechner himself notes that there are many ways of looking at this experience. He recognizes the possibility of psychological and sexual influences. He goes on to say that "looking back at those distant years I choose not to deny, either, the compelling sense of an unseen giver and a series of hidden gifts as not only another part of their reality, but the deepest part of all."

Many people have such experiences, researchers tell us, but not many people savor them and reflect on them and draw the implications of them for their lives. Ignatius did all these things. From such experiences and from his theological studies, he came to see that the universe is a place where God is continually drawing each and every one of us into the community life of the Trinity. It is as though the three Persons in God, the perfect community of Father, Son, and Holy Spirit, say to one another, "Our life in union is so rich and satisfying. Why don't we create a universe where we can invite other persons into our community life?"

Ignatius invites us to take seriously these foundational experiences of God creating us out of love and for a loving friendship with him. When we have such a relationship with God, we want nothing to get in its way, which is what Ignatius meant by the notion of being indifferent to all created things. It is not that we do not care for things, but rather that we do not want to be so attached to any of them that we miss the pearl of great price, which is to be in tune with God's purpose in creating the universe and each one of us.

Once our desire for a more intimate relationship with God is aroused, then we need to take time to let God draw us closer. Like the fox, we may feel a bit skittish with God. If so, we can tell God to take it slowly, so as not to frighten us off. Such a statement is a wonderfully honest prayer. We can also tell God that although we are somewhat fearful, we are attracted to a deeper relationship with him. In order to make time for God to draw us closer, we might take a page from the fox and set aside a particular time each day or week for the encounter with God. The time does not have to be long, but it is good to be regular—*Il faut des rites.* I would also suggest that we be clear about our desires, and about the ambivalence of our desires. Even though every human being is constantly being drawn by divine love toward union with God, still we all have conflicting desires as well. Fear gets in the way of our desire to become more intimate with God. Hurts from our past may leave us unsure if we can really trust God with our future. At this stage of our journey toward God, as at any stage, honesty is the best policy. Telling God about our deep ambivalence, and then listening for God's response, is part of the process of building the wall of friendship.

In these early stages of a developing intimacy with God, the rite of praying at a certain time, in a certain place, and in a certain manner is the scaffolding necessary for establishing a solid foundation for the friendship. Prayer books and books on prayer can also be helpful as scaffolding. In religious congregations, novitiates are places where structure and order are needed. They are the scaffolding necessary for building the wall that is a way of life. When the wall is built, then the scaffolding can gradually be allowed to fall away. So, too, in a developing relationship with God, when the ties are firmly established, the rites necessary at the beginning can be dropped. Indeed, a slavish holding on to the rites may be an indication that the relationship has not been well established. Ultimately, in our developing friendship with God, there comes a time when "we may let the scaffolds fall / Confident that we have built our wall."

## ❖ 2 ❖

# WHY WE PRAY

Some years ago, I attended a workshop on the relaxation response led by Herbert Benson, MD, a pioneer in mind/body medicine, and his associates. Dr. Benson has found that this response is the physiological opposite of the fight-or-flight response, in which, in times of perceived danger, the output of adrenaline leads to increased metabolism, blood pressure, respiration, and heart rate and faster brain waves. The opposite reactions—decreased blood pressure, respiration, and heart rate and slower brain waves—Benson calls the "relaxation response." Unlike the fight-or-flight response, which can lead to many physical and psychological illnesses if exposure is prolonged, the relaxation response has beneficial physical and psychological effects. Benson found that this response is induced by meditation, the kind taught by the Benedictine

John Main and his followers and called "centering prayer" by the Trappist M. Basil Pennington.

This workshop once again brought up for me the question, why do we pray? Do we pray for utilitarian reasons—because it benefits our physical or psychological health?

Honesty compels me to say that I often do pray for utilitarian reasons. First of all, most of my prayers of petition ask for some good result, either for me or for someone else or for all people. Moreover, I feel contented when I remember in prayer the people who mean much to me, even if my prayer is not answered. I notice, too, that I feel better about myself when I pray regularly. I feel more centered, more in tune with the present, less anxious about the past or the future. So I suspect that I do pray for the purpose of psychological or physical health. But does that exhaust my motivations for prayer?

Thinking of prayer as a conscious relationship, or friendship, with God may be illuminating. Why do we spend time with good friends? As I pondered this question, I realized that I relish times with good friends for some of the same reasons just adduced for spending time in prayer. If I have not had good conversations with close friends for some time, I feel out of sorts, somewhat lonely, and ill at ease. When I am with good friends, I feel more whole and alive. Still, I do not believe that my only reason for wanting time with them is to feel better. I want to be with them because I love them. I am genuinely interested in and concerned for them. The beneficial effect that being with them has on me is a happy by-product. Moreover, I have often spent time with friends when it cost me trouble and time, and I did it because they wanted my presence. Haven't we all spent time with a close friend who was ill or depressed, even when the time was painful and difficult? Such time spent cannot be explained on utilitarian grounds. We spend that time because we love our friend for his or her own sake.

Of course, there are times when we need the presence of close friends because we are in pain or lonely. Friendship would not be a mutual affair if we were always the ones who gave and never were open to receive. But if we are not totally egocentric, we will have to admit that we do care for others for their own sakes, and not just for what we can get from the relationship. We spend time with our friends because of our mutual care and love. Can we say the same thing about our relationship with God?

## Mutuality in Friendship with God

Before we look at the positive side of the analogy, let's notice where it limps, and badly. All human relationships, no matter how one-sided they may seem, are based on mutual need. To be anywhere near our best selves we need people who love us. As an infant, every one of us needs others to love and care for us. Without a caretaker we would die, and without a caretaker who shows care we would not develop as a person. Our dependence on others to be ourselves continues throughout life, even if that dependence lessens as we grow up. Even the parents upon whom the infant relies need the infant in some way, if only as the consummation of their love for each other. God, however, does not need anyone else. God—Father, Son, and Spirit—is the perfect community. They need nothing else for their completion. We must not succumb to the romantic notion that God decided to create a universe with other persons in it because God was lonely. God does not create out of need, but out of love.

Even though God does not create out of need, this does not mean that a relationship of mutuality is impossible. Such relationships are created by intention and desire as well as by need. Of course, I need my friends, but if my need is the prevailing motivation, then my fear of losing them will predominate over my love for them. So if we, with our neediness, establish friendships that are mutual, clearly God can do so. If God invites us into the community life of the Trinity, then God desires a relationship of mutuality with us.

The Hebrew Bible gives some indications of such an intention on God's part. In Genesis, we get the impression that before the Fall, God walked and conversed with Adam and Eve in the cool of the evening. We can also look at the Abraham stories in Genesis 12–18 as a saga of a growing mutual relationship between Abraham and God, culminating in God's decision to tell Abraham what God intends to do to Sodom and Gomorrah. God's revelation of the intention to destroy the cities leads Abraham to haggle with God to save them. Abraham goes so far as to tell God how he should act.

In the Gospel of John, Jesus tells his disciples (and through them, us): "I do not call you servants any longer, because the servant does not know what the master is doing; but I have called you friends, because I have made known to you everything that I have heard from my Father" (15:15). He goes on to underline his intention when he says: "You did not choose me but I chose you. And I appointed you to go and bear fruit, fruit that will last" (15:16). Throughout the history of Christianity, men and women have discovered, to their wonder and delight, that God wants an intimate mutual friendship with them.

Now, friendships of mutuality are characterized by mutual transparency. Jesus makes this clear in the passage from John's Gospel. He wants to be transparent to his friends. And what he reveals is his very intimate life of union with the Father and the Spirit. To Philip's request that Jesus show the disciples the Father, Jesus replies: "Have I been with you all this time, Philip, and you still do not know me? Whoever has seen me has seen the Father" (John 14:9). Throughout the last discourse in John's Gospel, Jesus reveals in a variety of ways his own inner life, culminating in the final prayer in chapter 17. Christians believe that Jesus is still revealing who he is and thus who God is to all those who are willing to pay attention. Ignatius of Loyola, for example, took it so much for granted that Jesus wants to reveal himself to us that he suggests that retreatants in the Second Week of the Spiritual Exercises ask for "an intimate knowledge of our Lord, who has become man for me, that I may love Him more and follow Him more closely" (n. 104).

It works the other way as well. People who take seriously the invitation to an intimate relationship with God find that God wants them to reveal themselves as well. God wants to know our hopes and dreams, our loves and hates, our fears and anxieties. What astounds us is that God seems to be pleased when we are transparent, even when what we reveal about ourselves seems unsavory or unsuitable to say. God does not stand on protocol with us. Our triune God seems delighted with our willingness to trust in God's desire for mutuality. Even when we tell God how angry we are with him, God listens with interest and sympathy. God desires to know us just as much as we desire to know God.

## WHY DO WE PRAY?

Prayer is a conscious relationship with God. Just as we spend time with friends because we love them and care for them, we spend time in prayer because we love God and want to be with God. Created out of love, we are drawn by the desire for "we know not what," for union with the ultimate Mystery, who alone will satisfy our deepest longing. That desire, we can say, is the Holy Spirit of God dwelling in our hearts, drawing us to the perfect fulfillment for which we were created—namely, community with the Trinity. That desire draws us toward a more and more intimate union with God.

We pray, then, at our deepest level, because we are drawn by the bonds of love. We pray because we love, and not just for utilitarian purposes. If prayer has beneficial effects—and

I believe that it does—that is because prayer corresponds to our deepest reality. When we are in tune with God, we cannot help but experience deep well-being. Ignatius of Loyola spoke of consolation as a sign of a person's being in tune with God's intention. But in the final analysis, the lover does not spend time with the Beloved because of the consolation; the lover just wants to be with the Beloved.

Another motive for prayer is the desire to praise and thank God because of his great kindness and mercy. In contemplating Jesus, we discover that God's love is not only creative but also overwhelmingly self-sacrificing. Jesus loved us even as we nailed him to the cross.

If we allow the desire for "we know not what" to draw us more and more into a relationship of mutual love with God, then we will, I believe, gradually take as our own that wonderful prayer so dear to St. Francis Xavier that begins *O Deus, ego amo te, nec amo te ut salves me*: "O God, I love you, and not because I hope for heaven thereby." Gerard Manley Hopkins translated the prayer:

> I love thee, God, I love thee—
> Not out of hope for heaven for me
> Nor fearing not to love and be
> In the everlasting burning.
> Thou, my Jesus, after me
> Didst reach thine arms out dying,
> For my sake sufferedst nails and lance,

Mocked and marred countenance,
Sorrows passing number,
Sweat and care and cumber,
Yea and death, and this for me,
And thou couldst see me sinning:
Then I, why should not I love thee,
Jesu so much in love with me?
Not for heaven's sake, not to be
Out of hell by loving thee;
Not for any gains I see;
But just the way that thou didst me
I do love and will love thee.
What must I love thee, Lord, for then?
For being my king and God. Amen.

## ❖ 3 ❖

# ATTRACTION AND RESISTANCE TO GOD

In the first two meditations, we noted that our deepest desire is for union with God, the perfect community of Father, Son, and Holy Spirit, and thus union with all other persons in that perfect community. Because God desires us into being in order that we may enjoy communion with God and with all persons, we desire this communion at the deepest level of our being.

The poet and cleric John Donne knew of this desire. His "Holy Sonnet 1" expresses it well:

Thou hast made me, and shall thy work decay?
Repair me now, for now mine end doth haste;
I run to death, and death meets me as fast,
And all my pleasures are like yesterday.
I dare not move my dim eyes any way,

Despair behind, and death before doth cast
Such terror, and my feeble flesh doth waste
By sin in it, which it towards hell doth weigh.
Only thou art above, and when towards thee
By thy leave I can look, I rise again;
But our old subtle foe so tempteth me,
That not one hour myself I can sustain.
Thy grace may wing me to prevent his art,
And thou like adamant draw mine iron heart.

If Donne had not experienced the strong desire for God, he would not have made such a vehement plea as we hear in the last line of the poem: "And thou like adamant draw mine iron heart." "Adamant" refers to the lodestone that acts as a magnet to iron. But the very fact that Donne speaks of his heart as "iron" reveals what the rest of the poem almost heartbreakingly expresses—namely, that there is something in him that prevents him from moving toward the desire of his heart. He refers to his feeble flesh, to his terror of death, to sin, and to the subtle foe as forces that keep him from his heart's desire. But even though he is resistant to the attraction to God, still his "iron heart" can be magnetized by God, the "adamant." Even in the midst of the deepest resistance, our hearts still are strongly attracted to God, so much so that we can beg God, as Donne does, to allure them.

The poet speaks for all of us who have tried to follow through on the deepest desire of our hearts. We all recognize that something gets in the way of our attaining this desire. The resistance is easy enough to understand when we do not have a positive image of God—for example, if God is experienced not as desirable but as an ogre or a judge. I have already indicated that people who have such an image of God need experiences of God as the benevolent and loving One who has desired each one of us into being. However, even those of us who have had such positive experiences of God are disconcerted, as was Donne, by our reluctance to follow up on these experiences. Even after a period of intense closeness to God, for example, we find ourselves unaccountably reluctant to engage in prayer the next day.

In a series of chapters in my book *Paying Attention to God*, I probe the sources of such resistance. Among them are our fear of the consequences of getting close to God ("What will God ask me to do?"), our fear of losing control of our lives to God (as though control were in our power), our fear of losing ourselves in the immensity of God, and our fear of death. Whatever the source, the resistance is real for anyone who takes the relationship with God seriously enough to pursue it actively.

St. Paul seems to have experienced the frustration of such resistance. In the letter to the Romans, he says, "I do not understand my own actions. For I do not do what I want, but I do the very thing I hate" (7:15) and goes on to say:

> So I find it to be a law that when I want to do what is good, evil lies close at hand. For I delight in the law

of God in my inmost self, but I see in my members
another law at war with the law of my mind, making
me captive to the law of sin that dwells in my members.
Wretched man that I am! Who will rescue me from this
body of death? (7:21–24)

I am sure that this passage resonates with all of us. Our deep
desire for God responds to the magnet pull of God's desire for
us, and yet we seem to do everything possible to demagne-
tize our hearts. We let our hearts become inordinately attached
to things that do not and cannot fulfill our deepest desire.
Money, reputation, family, alcohol and other substances, and
other people become more important than the pearl of great
price. These inordinate attachments are addictions that keep
us from what we most deeply want, but precisely because they
are addictions, we feel powerless to do anything about them.
Hence, Paul's cry of seeming despair: "Wretched man that I
am! Who will rescue me from this body of death?"

Paul answers his own question, or perhaps it is truer to
say that the question is answered for him: "Thanks be to God
through Jesus Christ our Lord!" (7:25). We are not powerless.
We can turn to a "higher power," as the Alcoholics Anonymous
program puts it. The very God who has made us for union with
the Trinity and with all persons makes it possible for us to
attain that union in spite of our resistance. Donne puts it thus:
"Only thou art above, and when towards thee / By thy leave I
can look, I rise again." God gives him the grace to look toward

God, and then, as it were, the magnetic pull of God draws him out of his despair.

But one time through the struggle is not the end of it. We will, it seems, carry our resistance to union with God to the grave. We wish that it could be over and done with at one fell swoop, but usually it is not to be. Again Paul gives us an example. In the midst of his "boasting" in the second letter to the Corinthians, he notes that "a thorn was given me in the flesh, a messenger of Satan to torment me, to keep me from being too elated" (12:7). We do not know what the thorn in his flesh was, but we can interpret it for our purposes as the ongoing resistance to the pull of God toward union. Paul goes on: "Three times I appealed to the Lord about this, that it would leave me, but he said to me, 'My grace is sufficient for you, for power is made perfect in weakness'" (12:8–9). In other words, we must continually rely on our "higher power," on the "adamant" who has made us for union and will not let us rest until we reach it.

In another powerful poem, "Holy Sonnet 14," John Donne describes the human dilemma in a series of paradoxes. It is a wonderful prayer for all of us who experience the pain of desiring God while at the same time resisting the magnetic power of God.

> Batter my heart, three-personed God; for you
> As yet but knock, breathe, shine, and seek to mend;
> That I may rise and stand, o'erthrow me, and bend

Your force to break, blow, burn, and make me new.
I, like an usurped town, to another due,
Labor to admit you, but O, to no end;
Reason, your viceroy in me, me should defend,
But is captived, and proves weak or untrue.
Yet dearly I love you, and would be loved fain,
But am betrothed unto your enemy.
Divorce me, untie or break that knot again;
Take me to you, imprison me, for I,
Except you enthrall me, never shall be free,
Nor ever chaste, except you ravish me.

## ❖ 4 ❖

# REJOICING IN GOD AMID SUFFERING

The brave words of Habakkuk 3:17–18 are regularly prayed by those who use the breviary for Morning Prayer:

> Though the fig tree does not blossom,
>     and no fruit is on the vines;
> though the produce of the olive fails
>     and the fields yield no food;
> though the flock is cut off from the fold
>     and there is no herd in the stalls,
> yet I will rejoice in the LORD;
>     I will exult in the God of my salvation.

In the midst of a devastating war against Israel, the prophet Habakkuk proclaims his faith in God. Some modern parallels might be a Jew professing such trust while awaiting transport to Auschwitz, or a Cambodian during the nightmare of the killing fields, or an Ethiopian during the latest drought. Those of us who pray this prayer in the comfort of our warmed rooms may miss the enormity of what we are saying. We may not even stop to ask ourselves whether such a prayer is mere whistling in the dark—believing in positive results even when circumstances are terribly bleak. Are such reassuring prayers opium for the people, as Marx would claim? In this meditation, I want to address this question by looking at the experiences that may lie behind such prayers.

## THEORY VERSUS EXPERIENCE

When we see the misery of those who face incurable wasting diseases, the devastation of war, and the horrors of starvation, do we think of rejoicing in the Lord? Looked at from the outside, such suffering and degradation seem absolutely foreign to the notion of joy or gratitude. Indeed, to suggest to someone suffering so horribly that he or she should thank God seems at best gratuitous, at worst insensitive and condescending. No sensible person tells a mother who has just lost her only child to leukemia to rejoice in the Lord. Indeed, so-called pastoral responses such as "God knows best" or "God has taken your baby to the realm of happiness" ring hollow and make me cringe. In the face of horror, silence and sympathy and a willingness just to be present seem the best pastoral responses. Theory has little to say at these junctures and often is an affront to the people who are facing such horrors.

The real question I would ask is whether Habakkuk was talking from theory or from experience. Since we cannot query him, perhaps we need to look to our own experiences or to the experiences of those who have suffered horribly. Do we experience joy in the midst of terrible sorrow and suffering? In effect, do we experience resurrection now? In his book *True Resurrection*, the Anglican theologian H. A. Williams makes the point that when "resurrection is considered in terms of past and future, it is robbed of its impact on the present." He argues strongly that the doctrine of the Resurrection, if it is to have a real impact on our lives, has to be based on present experience. He goes so far as to posit, "I have long felt that theological inquiry is basically related to self-awareness and that therefore it involves a process of self-discovery." In other words, theory about God has to be based on experience. Do we have experiences of resurrection right in the midst of our suffering and dying? Do we know people who have been able to pray the prayer of Habakkuk in the middle of their pain and loss?

Let's take the case of the Dutch Jew Etty Hillesum, who died in Auschwitz in 1943. Her diaries, written during the last two years of her life in the hell of Nazi-occupied Amsterdam, record an ever-deepening realization of the reality she and every Jew faced and, at the same time, an ever-deepening relationship with God, which seemed to give her great joy. At one point, she writes of the difficulty of understanding the evil that

God's creatures are capable of committing against one another. Yet, she says, she tries to face up to God's world as it is and continues to praise creation "despite everything."

As the certainty of the intention of the Nazis to exterminate all Jews grew in her, the willingness to confront reality also grew. In early July 1942, she wrote:

> Something has crystallized. I have looked our destruction, our miserable end, which has already begun in so many small ways in our daily life, straight in the eye and accepted it into my life, and my love of life has not been diminished. I am not bitter or rebellious, or in any way discouraged. . . . I have come to terms with life. . . .
>
> By "coming to terms with life" I mean: the reality of death has become a definite part of my life; my life has, so to speak, been extended by death, by my looking death in the eye and accepting it, by accepting destruction as part of life and no longer wasting my energies on fear of death or the refusal to acknowledge its inevitability. It sounds paradoxical: by excluding death from our life we cannot live a full life, and by admitting death into our life we enlarge and enrich it.

Here we see someone who faces the horrors of the reality surrounding her and yet can rejoice in the Lord. We have one example of someone who could pray and mean the prayer of Habakkuk.

Here is another example, from a poor black sharecropper from the American South called Nate Shaw who was put in jail for his involvement with the Sharecroppers Union in the 1930s. In the following excerpt from *All God's Dangers: The Life of Nate Shaw*, Shaw is an old man telling his story to author Theodore Rosengarten. Being poor and black, Shaw had no expectation of receiving justice. But in jail, something happened to him:

> All of a sudden, God stepped in my soul. Talk about hollerin and rejoicin, I just caught fire. My mind cleared up. I got so happy—I didn't realize where I was at. I lost sight on this world to a great extent. And the Master commenced a talkin to me just like a natural man. I heard these words plain . . . "Follow me and trust me for my holy righteous word." I just gone wild then, feelin a change. . . . Good God almighty, I just felt like I could have flown out the top of that jail. I commenced a shoutin bout the Lord, how good and kind and merciful He was. Freed my soul from sin. . . .
>
> Well, they had my trial and put me in prison. The Lord blessed my soul and set me in a position to endure it.

Obviously, Nate Shaw could have prayed the words of Habakkuk with feeling.

I have been privileged to be a spiritual director to many people. Two of them come to mind as I reflect with you on this topic of resurrection and our ability to trust in God in the midst of horror. Both have given me permission to use their stories in this meditation.

One woman came to a deep sympathy for the sufferings of Jesus on the cross. Contemplation of Jesus on the cross brought her great pain and an acute sense of the suffering of the poor and sick people to whom she ministered. Yet she wanted nothing more than to be close to Jesus, in spite of the pain such closeness caused her.

During this period of intense contemplation of Jesus on the cross, she became aware, for the first time, of how she had been seriously abused in her childhood. These memories flooded her consciousness and led to feelings of pain and outrage and horror that she could hardly bear. Yet through it all, she felt a deep sense of being held in the loving embrace of a mothering God, an experience that brought her great consolation. If she tried to evade the memories or repress them, then this consoling presence of God also left her. It became clear to both of us that she could not experience true resurrection without experiencing what she was being resurrected from. She could, without pretense, pray the prayer of Habakkuk. Indeed, she could come to the point of accepting all that had happened to her as what had made her who she now was, a resurrected daughter of a loving God.

Another woman rediscovered God in the midst of terrible suffering brought on by treatment for Hodgkin's disease. As she described her experience, it seemed to be one of deep joy and freedom in the depths of pain and suffering and of loss of control over her own life. She told me that she would not wish not to have had the disease. Recently, she wrote to me that this experience of God had returned. She described it this way:

> I have had [the experience of God] back again this fall. It finally came to me, with blinding simplicity, that I should let my friends help me. And in accepting openheartedly what was offered unreservedly, I was rewarded with received grace, that sense of being filled up with light, of seeing truly, of being fully conscious, of being free: completely engaged with the world, yet not bound to it. Surprised by joy. How slowly, how tentatively we learn, over and over, to surrender to God's love! Perhaps this is why we humans [need to] live such long lives.

Do we not hear in these lines echoes of "Though the fig tree does not blossom . . . / yet I will rejoice in the LORD"?

These examples show that it is possible to find deep consolation at the heart of deep suffering. It is possible to rejoice in the Lord in spite of—or, indeed, because of—all the sufferings human life is heir to. But they also show that such "received grace" is not cheap grace. The person who can say with the psalmist, "Even though I walk through the darkest valley, / I fear no evil; / for you are with me; / your rod and your staff— / they comfort me" (23:4) knows that this comfort is given precisely in the valley of the shadow of death and nowhere else at this particular time in his or her life. Mary Ward, a seventeenth-century nun, once said, "The pain is great, but very endurable, because he who lays on the burden also carries it."

When we contemplate Jesus on the cross, we come to the depth of the mystery of God's love for us, of God's reckless gamble to draw us into the community life that is Father, Son, and Holy Spirit. For me, two of the last utterances of Jesus capture the mystery of the one event that is death-resurrection: "Eli, Eli, lema sabachthani?"—"My God, my God, why have you forsaken me?" (Matthew 27:46)—expresses the deep pain of the Crucifixion, while "Father, into your hands I commend my spirit" (Luke 23:46) expresses Jesus' ultimate trust that all is well. In the appearance to the two disciples on the road to Emmaus, Jesus conveys something to which all the people whose experiences I have adduced would agree: "Was it not necessary that the Messiah should suffer these things and then enter into his glory?" (Luke 24:26). Jesus would not be the Messiah he now is if his life had taken a different turn. Perhaps we cannot experience the fullness of resurrection as long as we harbor resentments about what life has dealt us. Perhaps we cannot experience resurrection until, like the woman who rediscovered God, we ask for the help we need and surrender wholeheartedly to God.

## ❖ 5 ❖

# HAPPINESS IN KNOWING
# WHAT PLEASES GOD

In the Old Testament, we often read that the people of God are blessed because they know the law of the Lord. This fragment from the book of Baruch is only one of many instances:

> Happy are we, O Israel,
>> for we know what is pleasing to God.
>>> (4:4)

Another comes from the book of Nehemiah. After the Israelites return from exile, they beg Ezra to read from the book of the law of Moses. He reads to them for the whole morning. "And all the people went their way to eat and drink and to send portions and to make great rejoicing, because they had understood the words that were declared to them" (8:12). The psalmist waxes eloquent on the wonders of knowing and obeying the law:

> I delight in the way of your decrees
>   as much as in all riches.
> I will meditate on your precepts,
>   and fix my eyes on your ways.
> I will delight in your statutes;
>   I will not forget your word.
>   (119:14–16).

Some time ago, when I read the passage from Baruch in the Liturgy of the Hours, I asked myself whether it is true that the Israelites are blessed to know what pleases God, that we Christians are blessed because of such knowledge. Are you really happier because you know the law of the Lord?

I remembered a story told to me by an old friend from my scholastic days in Germany. Adolph is now a Jesuit priest working in Indonesia. One time on his way to the States, he stopped in Thailand, where there has been religious tolerance for hundreds of years. He asked a missionary with many years of experience in Thailand why there were so few Christians in a country where there was relative freedom to preach the gospel. The missionary replied that the Thai people are a happy and contented people; if they were to become Christian, they would have to obey all the laws of the church. Adolph hit his head with his hand and exclaimed, "So much for the Good News." I wonder how many of us have thought at times that we would have an easier time of it if we were not Christians or Roman Catholics. Is knowledge of what pleases God really good news?

In today's world, it does not always seem so. Take, for instance, our liturgies. To be truthful, we would have to admit that a stranger visiting most of our liturgical "celebrations" would wonder about our use of language. We do not look as though we are enjoying ourselves or celebrating anything. How many of us go regularly to the Sunday liturgy because we feel that we have to go—in other words, because we know what pleases God? If we did not "have to" go, would we? In my work as a spiritual director, I have met many people whose prayer brings them no sense of being blessed. When asked why they continue to try to pray, they answer, "Because I have to, because God wants me to."

Apparently, knowing what pleases God does not make everyone feel happy. Some people who live very "religious" lives do not exude a sense of happiness. A nursing nun, it was reported to me, once told a woman in labor that her pains were just recompense for the pleasure of sex. It does not seem as though the nun's renunciation of marriage and family made her feel happy. Scrupulous people suffer a great deal in trying to fulfill the least letter of the law; there is no joy in their hearts that they know what pleases God. A friend of mine once told me that he had come to the point of hating God for making him stay in religious life; he thought that being a religious was what would please God. I was relieved when someone I was directing finally told me that he hated to pray and hated the God who seemed to demand that he pray, because I felt that we had at last touched reality and that now he could move forward in his relationship with God.

The knowledge that Baruch speaks of must mean more than a grudging acceptance of the will of God if it is to lead to blessedness. Those who obey the will of God grudgingly usually are not happy and very often seem holier-than-thou, looking down on those who do not live up to their high standards. If Scripture is to be believed, knowledge of what is pleasing to God and an attempt to live according to that knowledge should lead to humility, gentleness, gratitude, and joy. Does it?

## EXPERIENCES OF BLESSEDNESS IN DOING WHAT PLEASES GOD

The question cannot be answered in the abstract or by theory. It can only be answered by each one of us from our experience. Before I give some examples of a positive answer to the question, let me pose another question: Does it make sense to expect to feel blessed in this life at all? Again, one is tempted to answer that it does not make sense. The central Christian symbol is the cross; Jesus suffered this horrible and demeaning death because he knew what pleases God and acted accordingly. Certainly, he was blessed afterward in the Resurrection, but could anyone honestly say that he was blessed during the Crucifixion? This life is a vale of tears, and those who know what pleases God and act according to that knowledge often suffer just as Jesus suffered. There was an unspoken rule for discernment prevalent in the church prior to Vatican II that the more unpalatable of two choices was the one to lean toward, since it was more likely in accord with God's will. The idea that we should expect to feel happy in this life seems far-fetched, does it not?

And yet, in the rules for discernment of spirits proposed by Ignatius of Loyola in *The Spiritual Exercises*, we read that for those "who go on earnestly striving to cleanse their souls from sin and who seek to rise in the service of God,"

> it is characteristic of the good spirit . . . to give cour-age and strength, consolations, tears, inspirations, and peace. This He does by making all easy, by removing all obstacles so that the soul goes forward in doing good. (n. 315)

Ignatius expects that those who know what pleases God and act accordingly will be blessed. And Ignatius is talking from experience—his own and others'—not from theory.

According to him, if we are trying to live a life in accor-dance with God's good pleasure, the best criterion for decid-ing whether an experience or a choice or a way of acting is of God or not is to ask whether we find ourselves "blessed," in the sense of having "courage and strength, consolations, tears, inspirations, and peace." This rule echoes Paul's words to the

Galatians based on his own experiences: "The fruit of the Spirit is love, joy, peace, patience, kindness, generosity, faithfulness, gentleness, and self-control" (5:22–23). In fact, in the same rule Ignatius notes that "it is characteristic of the evil spirit to harass with anxiety, to afflict with sadness, to raise obstacles backed by fallacious reasonings that disturb the soul." From his experience, Ignatius, it seems, would echo the words of Baruch with which we began this meditation.

In the Sermon on the Mount, Jesus himself proclaimed as blessed the poor in spirit, the brokenhearted, the meek, those who hunger and thirst for righteousness, the merciful, the pure in heart, the peacemakers, and even the persecuted (Matthew 5:3–11). Jesus was proclaiming not a theory but a fact, a fact born out by his experience. On the cross he did suffer terribly; his cry of anguish, "My God, my God, why have you forsaken me?" (Matthew 27:46), has chilled many Christians to the marrow as they contemplated this scene in prayer. Yet whatever the meaning of this cry, Jesus was still able to say, "Father, forgive them; for they do not know what they are doing" (Luke 23:34) and, with his final breath, "Father, into your hands I commend my spirit" (23:46). Such words could not come from a person who was not somehow blessed and thus able to think of others and to trust his Father. It would appear that Jesus himself experienced happiness in knowing what pleases God.

In the Acts of the Apostles, we read that Peter and the other apostles were flogged by the Sanhedrin and told not to speak in the name of Jesus. "As they left the council, they rejoiced that they were considered worthy to suffer dishonor for the sake of the name. And every day in the temple and at home they did not cease to teach and proclaim Jesus as the Messiah" (5:41–42). Often in his letters, Paul attests to his joy in being able to suffer for the sake of the gospel. For example, in the second letter to the Corinthians, he says, "So, I will boast all the more gladly of my weaknesses, so that the power of Christ may dwell in me. Therefore I am content with weaknesses, insults, hardships, persecutions, and calamities for the sake of Christ; for whenever I am weak, then I am strong" (12:9–10). Apparently, in the early church, knowing what pleases God and acting according to that knowledge did bring a sense of blessedness.

Down the centuries, people have found blessedness from knowing what pleases God and acting according to this knowledge even when their actions led to their suffering and martyrdom. St. Lawrence, the deacon who was burned to death, is reputed to have kept his sense of humor even in his last agony. St. Ignatius of Antioch could not wait to be torn to pieces by the lions and hoped that nothing would prevent him from his martyrdom. St. Francis of Assisi rejoiced in being considered a fool for Christ. St. Ignatius of Loyola felt deep consolation when he was imprisoned by the inquisitors. In these cases and others, the blessedness seems to have come from a deep love of and deep identification with Jesus. Because of their great love of Jesus and their desire to follow Jesus in knowing and doing what pleases God, they discovered their deepest happiness. They were indeed blessed.

In more recent times, we have instances of ordinary people who have known and done what pleases God and found blessedness, even in very hard circumstances. Etty Hillesum, the young Dutch Jewish woman mentioned in the last meditation, testifies in her diaries to the grace of blessedness given in the worst of circumstances. The more she came to know and live out what pleases God, the more peaceful and happy she became. Three months before her death, while being held at Westerbork, a concentration camp in the Netherlands, she wrote in her diary, "You have made me so rich, oh God, please let me share out Your beauty with open hands."

Archbishop Oscar Romero, two weeks before he was murdered for speaking about what pleases God, said:

> Martyrdom is a grace from God that I do not believe I have earned. . . . May my death, if it is accepted by God, be for the liberation of my people. . . . You can tell them, if they succeed in killing me, that I pardon them.

These and many others like them seem to have been brought by the grace of God and their relationship with Jesus to the point where they were already living the resurrected life of Jesus. With the risen Christ, they lived, as Sebastian Moore puts it in *Jesus the Liberator of Desire*, no longer "under the shadow of death" but "in the light with death behind" them. "The virus of eternity" had entered their "bloodstream forever."

These are examples of people who have found blessedness even in the most harrowing of circumstances by knowing and following what pleases God. But what of us ordinary folk who try to live a Christian life? Do we find happiness in knowing and doing what pleases God? I leave the answer to each of you. For myself, I have to say what I said many years ago when a group of Jesuits were arguing about the merits of living a religious life with vows of poverty, chastity, and obedience. I became irritated with the utilitarian arguments for the religious life and blurted out something like this: "I believe that God wants me to be a Jesuit for my happiness and good, and I am very grateful to God for this." Now, over forty years later, I can still say that I feel blessed that I know and am trying to do what pleases God. It seems to me that knowing and doing what pleases God is also what most pleases me at the deepest level of my being. Does that sound right to you?

## ❖ 6 ❖

# THE FUNDAMENTAL CHRISTIAN VIRTUE OF GRATITUDE

In an article, I once suggested that there are some people too traumatized by early life crises to be able to shift the focus from themselves to others. Such people, I opined, would be incapable of entering the stage of the spiritual journey that is called discipleship, or the following of Jesus. In Ignatian terms, these people could not move beyond the First Week of the Spiritual Exercises.

I referred to the man from whom the legion of demons had been driven. When he wanted to follow Jesus, Jesus denied his request, saying, "Go home to your friends, and tell them how much the Lord has done for you, and what mercy he has shown you" (Mark 5:19). These lines, for some readers, may raise the specter of a caste in Christianity, of another distinction between real Christians and the also-rans. Truth to tell, some of the rhetoric of the literature on vocations to the priesthood and religious life gives the impression that there are two classes of Christians, which can lead to a belief that one is better than the other. In the meditation at hand, I want to address this issue. I suggest that gratitude is the appropriate attitude for any Christian, and that it will keep any of us from taking a holier-than-thou stance toward others.

The man from whom the legion of demons was driven out did not ask to be possessed by demons. Children with Down syndrome do not bring on their condition. Battered and sexually abused children cannot be blamed for what has happened to them. Moreover, if we have escaped being afflicted in any of these ways, we cannot take credit for it. Whenever we see someone afflicted, the only appropriate response is sympathy for him or her and the realization that "there but for the grace of God go I." Indeed, since we do not know the mind of God, perhaps the most appropriate response is just gratitude for life and all it brings, without any comparisons. Who knows whether it is better to be born without Down syndrome than with it? At the least, I want to raise the question for reflection.

## Gratitude without Comparisons

In her short story "Revelation," Flannery O'Connor tells of a day in the life of a Southern lady, Mrs. Turpin. In the course of a visit to the doctor, she has occasion to congratulate herself a number of times on her superiority to those she encounters in the office. At the end of the story, she has some kind of a revelation. She sees a vast swinging bridge on which a mass of people are making their way to heaven. Leading the way are hordes of people whom Mrs. Turpin always considered beneath her—"white-trash" people, blacks, and "freaks and lunatics"— "shouting and clapping and leaping like frogs."

> And bringing up the end of the procession was a tribe of people whom she recognized at once as those who, like herself and Claud, had always had a little of everything and the God-given wit to use it right. . . . They were marching behind the others with great dignity, accountable as they had always been for good order and common sense and respectable behavior. They alone were on key. Yet she could see by their shocked and altered faces that even their virtues were being burned away.

Mrs. Turpin discovers in this revelation that all of us human beings are equal in the sight of God. I suppose that the "tribe of people" like herself and Claud became more and more grateful as "their virtues were being burned away." As they were being transformed, I wonder if they made any comparisons at all, even in their gratitude. Remember that the Pharisee prayed in comparative form: "God, I thank you that I am not like other people: thieves, rogues, adulterers, or even like this tax collector. I fast twice a week; I give a tenth of all my income." The tax collector to whom the Pharisee is compared prays without comparison: "God, be merciful to me, a sinner!" (Luke 18:11–13).

In the parable of the sower (Matthew 13:1–9), Jesus speaks of the seed that falls on good soil and produces a crop. Notice that the crop produced can be a hundred, sixty, or thirty times what was sown. In his explanation of the parable, Jesus does not imply that one yield is better than another; no matter what the yield, "what was sown on good soil, this is the one who hears the word and understands it" (13:23). According to this parable, all we need to do is open our hearts to the grace of God and let God take care of what harvest will be produced. Our gifts and talents differ, and as a result the harvest produced will differ. But such differences do not make some people better in the eyes of God. Whatever talents or gifts we have are just that—gifts. And gratitude is the only proper response to the reception of gifts.

Gratitude for what we are given runs counter to the competitive nature of our culture. From infancy, we are taught to compare ourselves with others in terms of talent or looks. IQ tests, SAT scores, class rankings—all compel us to compare ourselves with others. In such a culture, the inability to do what others can do and are applauded for can lead to a sense of inferiority. Hence, the man from whom the legion of demons was cast out would, in our culture, tend to think of himself as less valued by Jesus than the apostles who get to follow him. Under such circumstances, the Christian attitude of gratitude and acceptance of the gifts one has does not come easily. We need to pray regularly and often for gratitude to God for who we are.

Perhaps even more important is to pray to know in our bones that we are the apple of God's eye just as we are. Once, a retreatant felt that Jesus was telling him, "I love no one more than I love you, but I don't love you more than anyone else." This was a consoling experience for him and left him feeling very grateful. Moreover, he had no basis for making comparative judgments about his worth in the eyes of Jesus. What a great relief and freedom it would be if we could believe that Jesus makes no comparisons but loves each of us as we are, and wants the best for each of us.

If we are given this grace, then we will also be rid of the kinds of feelings of inferiority that lead to envy, comparative judgments, and a sense that the call of some people to follow Jesus as priests or religious makes them better Christians. St. Paul must have had such a grace and then realized how free it made him. Hence, he could insist so strongly that no one can boast except in the cross of Christ, that all of us are parts of the one body of Christ, and that each of us needs to play our role in building up the body:

> But God has so arranged the body, giving the greater honor to the inferior member, that there may be no dissension within the body, but the members may have

the same care for one another. If one member suffers, all suffer together with it; if one member is honored, all rejoice together with it.

Now you are the body of Christ and individually members of it. And God has appointed in the church first apostles, second prophets, third teachers; then deeds of power, then gifts of healing, forms of assistance, forms of leadership, various kinds of tongues. Are all apostles? Are all prophets? Are all teachers? Do all work miracles? Do all possess gifts of healing? Do all speak in tongues? Do all interpret? But strive for the greater gifts. (1 Corinthians 12:24–31)

As we know, Paul then swings into his famous hymn to love. Gratitude for the gift of who we are and have become by the grace of God does lead quite naturally into love.

Part 2

# Paradoxes

# 7

# FEAR AND FAITH

Fear sits deep within each one of us. We are afraid of so many things: the dark, the discovery of our secret fault or flaw, sickness, pain, loss of money or prestige or reputation, loss of our loved ones, death itself. Fear keeps us from trusting other people, from trying new things, even from enjoying life. I venture to say that fear may be *the* manifestation of original sin in our lives. Because of fear, we find it very difficult to live out the dream of God for our universe—that it be a place where all people live in harmony with the perfect community that is the triune God and with one another.

In this meditation, I want to explore our fear and its implications for the life of faith. Seamus Heaney, in his poem entitled "Storm on an Island," sets the stage:

We are prepared: we build our houses squat.
Sink walls in rock and roof them with good slate.
This wizened earth has never troubled us
With hay, so, as you see, there are no stacks
Or stooks that can be lost. Nor are there trees
Which might prove company when it blows full
Blast: you know what I mean—leaves and branches
Can raise a tragic chorus in a gale
So that you listen to the thing you fear
Forgetting that it pummels your house too.
But there are no trees, no natural shelter.
You might think that the sea is company,
Exploding comfortably down on the cliffs
But no: when it begins, the flung spray hits
The very windows, spits like a tame cat
Turned savage. We just sit tight while wind dives
And strafes invisibly. Space is a salvo,
We are bombarded by the empty air.
Strange, it is a huge nothing that we fear.

The "huge nothing" that we fear in Heaney's poem is the air. But his poem can provide us with food for thought. Is it a huge nothing that we fear? In other words, should we fear at all?

On the face of things, it seems it is a huge *something* that we fear. The people who live on the Aran Islands have good reason to fear the storms that regularly beat upon them; it would be foolhardy not to. It is right for parents to teach their children to fear fire and bare electric wires, oncoming traffic, vicious dogs. Given the daily headlines, parents have good reason to instill in their children a healthy fear of strangers, especially if they offer them rides. It is only sensible to be afraid of the loss of all means of support for oneself and one's family. Dire poverty, debilitating sickness, and cruel suffering are not great boons. And death deprives us of the refreshing and consoling presence of our loved ones.

A good case can be made for the contention that Jesus considered fear the opposite of faith—that he would therefore have agreed with Heaney. In the Gospels, Jesus equates lack of faith not with failure to believe in doctrine but with fear. In the Sermon on the Mount, he tells us not to worry about what we will eat or drink or how we will clothe ourselves, that those who worry about such things are people "of little faith" (Matthew 6:30). When the disciples rouse Jesus during the storm at sea, he says, "Why are you afraid? Have you still no faith?" (Mark 4:40). In another storm at sea, Jesus comes to the disciples walking on the water. Again his message is "Do not be afraid." When Peter begins to walk on the water toward Jesus, fear takes over, and Peter begins to sink. Jesus saves him and then asks, "You of little faith, why did you doubt?" (Matthew 14:31). Before this incident, when Jesus tells the disciples that they will be flogged and arrested, he adds, "When they hand you over, do not worry about how you are to speak or what you are to say; for what you are to say will be given to you at that time; for it is not you who speak, but the Spirit of your

Father speaking through you" (Matthew 10:19–20), and later, "So do not be afraid; you are of more value than many sparrows" (10:31). From this sampling of Jesus' words, we can draw the conclusion that the opposite of faith is fear, that fear and faith are incompatible.

In these passages, the disciples are faced with many of the common fears of the human race. We fear that there will not be enough of the goods of this world to go around and that we will go hungry or thirsty or unclothed. We fear the unknown and so tend to avoid anything new or unexpected. We fear the loss of our reputation or our good name if we take a stand for what is right against the weight of public opinion. We fear, above all, pain, suffering, and death. Jesus tells us that all these fears reveal our lack of faith.

Now we return to the earlier question. To fear poverty, loss of our good name, or arrest and death seems only reasonable. No sensible person would, for example, give up his or her health or life insurance, and isn't the provision of such insurance precisely to keep fear at bay? Does the faith Jesus demands mean that job security, social security, health and life insurance, and savings for a rainy day are to be relinquished? At one point in the Gospel, when Jesus says how hard it is for a rich person to enter the kingdom of heaven, the disciples ask in amazement, "Then who can be saved?" (Matthew 19:25). We may feel the same amazement.

Jesus' answer may point us in a more hopeful direction: "For mortals it is impossible, but for God all things are possible" (Matthew 19:26). Apparently, God can make up for our lack of faith and thus bring us home safely to the kingdom in spite of the fears that bind us.

I would also say that the issue is not whether we have social security or job security, but whether we put our trust in these frail treasures to the point that we are paralyzed by fear when they are threatened.

## INORDINATE ATTACHMENTS AND INDIFFERENCE

These reflections lead us to look at what happens when we do put our trust in the security measures we have taken for ourselves and our loved ones. The story of the rich young man can serve as an illustration. He was a good man, one who kept all the commandments.

> Jesus, looking at him, loved him and said, "You lack one thing; go, sell what you own, and give the money to the poor, and you will have treasure in heaven; then come, follow me." When he heard this, he was shocked and went away grieving, for he had many possessions. (Mark 10:21–22)

The poignancy in the story comes in the last line: he "went away grieving." Because of his inordinate attachment to his wealth, he cannot have what he really wants, close companionship with Jesus. When we put too much of our trust in security measures, reputation, wealth, or degrees, we cannot really be happy. Worse yet, we cannot enjoy the very things we covet, because we fear their loss so much. Think of the jealous lover who constantly agonizes about whether the beloved reciprocates his love.

Aren't the people we see whose faces radiate an inner happiness and peace those who are not attached inordinately to what they have or what they have achieved? Near the end of his life, Ignatius of Loyola was described as full of life and radiating an inner joy. One reason for his inner joy could have been that he did not fear the loss of anything he held dear. He told one companion that if the pope should dissolve the Society of Jesus, it would take Ignatius only fifteen minutes to attain serenity. In his *Autobiography*, he also says that in his last years the thought of his impending death gave him such joy that he dissolved into tears. Obviously, he loved the Society of Jesus and his life, but he had been brought by grace to the point where he was not inordinately attached to either of them. And so he was an eminently happy man.

Pedro Arrupe, the late father general of the Jesuits, told this story of celebrating Mass in one of the poorest slums of a city in Latin America:

> The Mass was held in a small, open building in very poor repair; there was no door, and dogs came and went freely. Mass began with hymns accompanied by a guitarist, and the result was marvelous. The words

of the hymn went: "Love is giving of oneself, forgetting oneself, while seeking what will make others happy. . . ." As the hymn continued I felt a lump in my throat. I had to make a real effort to continue the Mass. These people seemed to possess nothing and yet they were ready to give of themselves to communicate joy and happiness.

After Mass, a big man invited Arrupe to come to his place. At first, Arrupe was reluctant to accept, but he was encouraged by one of the priests and went. The man's place was a hovel ready to collapse.

He had me sit down on a rickety old chair. From there I could see the sunset. The big man said to me, "Look, sir, how beautiful it is!" We sat in silence for several minutes. The sun disappeared. The man then said, "I don't know how to thank you for all you have done for us. I have nothing to give you, but I thought you would like to see this sunset. You liked it, didn't you? Good evening."

Every time I read this story, a lump comes to my throat and tears to my eyes. Here is a man who really is poor in spirit and blessed.

Perhaps the only way that we can really enjoy what we have is not to fear its loss. And that includes health, vitality, the goods of this world, friends, and life itself.

In the Principle and Foundation of *The Spiritual Exercises*, Ignatius indicates that a profound experience of God as the only true satisfaction of our deepest desires can lead us to what he calls indifference toward all other things. "Indifference" does not mean not caring about other people or things, but "being at a balance toward," or "not being inordinately attached to," all other persons and things. As previously noted, this experience of the desire for God, or for "we know not what," is what C. S. Lewis calls joy, a desire that is more fulfilling and delightful than the possession of any good. In thrall to this desire, we will be able, as Ignatius puts it, not to "prefer health to sickness, riches to poverty, honor to dishonor, a long life to a short life." We only want "what is more conducive to the end for which we are created," which is union with the triune God. Perhaps, then, the Beatitudes are the truest of all the sayings of Jesus, because only those who love God more than anything else can be truly blessed. Only those who have the faith Jesus spoke of, the faith that is the opposite of fear, can really say and mean, "Blessed are the poor in spirit. . . . Blessed are those who mourn. . . . Blessed are the meek. . . . Blessed are those who are persecuted for righteousness' sake" (Matthew 5:3–10).

Of course, none of us can attain the "indifference" that is a prerequisite to blessedness by willing it. Our hearts, at their most profound levels, may desire union with the triune God, but we also know that at other levels we desire many other things, and that these desires are not usually ordered, but disordered and inordinate. What can we do to attain true happiness? We can beg God to help us get our hearts in order; we can pay attention to the movements of our hearts and minds and begin to discern which of these movements are for our peace. In other words, we can learn by trial and error and the grace of God what we really and most profoundly want and take the steps that will lead us in that direction. The Spiritual Exercises of Ignatius are one means to this blessed end. At any rate, if we want to be blessed, if we want to enjoy life and the goods of this life in any meaningful way, we need to come to believe deep in our hearts that "it is a huge nothing that we fear."

# 8

# BE NOT AFRAID

Some years ago, when I was making my annual retreat at Miramar Retreat Center, in Duxbury, Massachusetts, I spent some time watching a goose family, parents and five goslings. The goslings were already rather well formed, but they could not yet stretch out their necks as the adults could to see all around them. As I got to know the habits of the geese, I realized that the goslings did not have to be on the alert. Wherever they went, one of the parents was in the lead, for the most part keeping an eye out for what lay ahead. The other parent usually walked behind, its neck extended to its full length, seemingly alert for danger from any direction. Whenever the family was feeding on the grass, one of the adults would appear to stand guard, with its neck extended. The goslings did not have to be afraid, I observed, because they were always under the protection of their parents.

Is it possible that this family of geese can teach us a lesson about how we might live life without being overcome by fear? I believe it can.

Of course, we might object that these goslings are too dumb to be afraid. All they want is to fill their bellies, and the means are at hand. So they go their merry way, just munching away without a care in the world. But I noticed that whenever one or another got too far behind the lead parent, the gosling would flap its wings and move to catch up with the crowd. I got the impression that the goslings were aware of the presence of their parents, especially of the one who led them. When the parents seemed to be absent, the goslings appeared to show fear and did what they could to get back to the safety of their parents' presence. When Jesus wanted to encourage his disciples not to be afraid, he said: "Look at the birds of the air; they neither sow nor reap nor gather into barns, and yet your heavenly Father feeds them. Are you not of more value than they?" (Matthew 6:26). Perhaps our goose family, birds mostly of the ground and the water, can help us further deepen Jesus' analogy.

In the Gospels, there are two different storms at sea. In one, Jesus is in the boat, but asleep, when the storm hits. The disciples are terrified and wake Jesus up, and he calms the storm (see Luke 8:22–25). In the second, the disciples are alone in the boat during the storm and suddenly see Jesus walking toward them on the water. They think it is a ghost and are terrified. Are they not like the goslings when they become aware of the absence of their parents? The disciples are terrified because Jesus seems absent; but in the presence of Jesus, there is nothing to fear. Indeed, that seems to be the message Jesus tries to inculcate in them: "Take heart, it is I; do not be afraid" (Mark 6:50). Do we have similar experiences? I can say for myself that my anxieties and fears usually run rampant when I am out of touch with the presence of Jesus, the Father, or the Holy Spirit.

Rarely, thank God, I cannot sleep. Usually, it is because something is bothering me and I cannot get it off my mind. I try to rationalize it away with reassuring thoughts: "No one noticed that faux pas anyway." I get into imaginary conversations in which I explain how I was in the right and the other person in the wrong. I try to think of something else. Nothing works, and so I toss and turn in fear and anxiety. At these moments, I try to put my trust in God, but even that does not work. Sometimes exhaustion sets in, and I sleep fitfully. When I reflect on these times, I realize that even my "prayer" is somewhat desperate and that I do not have a felt sense of the presence of God. More recently, I have found that trying to tell God how I feel, even when I do not have a sense of God's presence, gradually begins to help. I begin to quiet down and recognize that I am making a mountain out of a molehill, that in the large scheme of things what I am worrying about is small change. Like the goslings in the presence of their parents, I have been freed of fear by the felt presence of Jesus, of God, of the Holy Spirit.

Now, this experience does not automatically make everything better thereafter. I believe that we have to cultivate a sense of the presence of God in our daily lives to be able to live without being controlled by fear. We cannot control our fears in healthy ways by willing ourselves to believe in God's presence. We need to experience that presence in a profound way. Like the goslings, we need that felt presence to become second nature.

Here I can only suggest that it takes practice on our part, practice in paying attention to God's presence in our daily lives. I suppose that anyone who reads a book like this attempts such a practice. It is important to note that trying too hard to become aware of the presence of God may be counterproductive. It might be more conducive to a growing awareness of that presence to take a few moments each day to reflect on the past day, asking God's help to see when we were most alive and living in the present moment, when we were not worrying about the past or the future. In these moments, I believe, we are aware of the mystery of the moment and of the mysterious Stranger who makes our hearts burn within us (see Luke 24:32). Often, too, when we are anxious and feeling lost, we can allow the Lord to touch us with his calming presence by doing something "contemplative," like smelling coffee or a rose, watching the sun on a tree or a family of geese, listening to music or to birds, feeling the breeze. Such contemplative activities allow the Spirit to make her presence felt.

It may be argued that the goslings are living in a dream-world if they believe that staying in the presence of their parents will shield them from all harm: on the contrary, they could be shot by a hunter, snared by a hawk, poisoned by herbicides. This is true enough, and we could say the same about our own confidence and peace in the presence of God. Trust in God's presence will not keep us from being mugged on city streets, from contracting cancer, from experiencing bereavement and death. Jesus' trust in God did not prevent him from being tortured and crucified.

Here again, the goslings may tell us something. Suppose that they were aware of the possibility of sudden and painful suffering and death in spite of the presence of their parents. What good would it do to worry about this possibility? Such worry would do nothing but spoil the enjoyment they have in the presence of their parents. So, too, if we worry about all the bad things that could happen to us and try to shield ourselves at all costs against such eventualities, then we will live always in fear, and that is hell indeed. When Jesus says to his disciples, "Take heart, it is I; do not be afraid," he is not guaranteeing that they will never suffer and die, only that he will be with them—and us. For those who have experienced that presence, it is enough—indeed, more than enough.

Let me end with a wonderful aphorism of the late Scottish philosopher John Macmurray, which I cite often in my writing and repeat even more to myself.

> All religion . . . is concerned to overcome fear. We can distinguish real religion from unreal by contrasting their formulae for dealing with negative motivation. The maxim of illusory religion runs: "Fear not; trust in God and he will see that none of the things you fear will happen to you"; that of real religion, on the contrary, is "Fear not; the things that you are afraid of are quite likely to happen to you, but they are nothing to be afraid of."

## ❖ 9 ❖

# APPEARANCE AND REALITY

Pilate asked him, "So you are a king?" Jesus answered,
"You say that I am a king."

—John 18:37

We have heard these words so often that we may not detect the
incongruity. Jesus was arrested the evening before and brought
before the Sanhedrin, where he was accused of crimes worthy
of death. He might have a black eye from the blow to the face
he received from one of the servants of the high priest. He has
been up all night, part of the time being mocked by the guards.
His clothes might be torn and dirty and covered with spittle
and spots of his own blood. He probably smells bad. One way
to read Pilate's words is as an astonished "*You*, a king? You look
more like a common criminal or a bum." The only time in

Jesus' life when it would have been more incongruous to call him a king would be on the cross itself. Yet, at this nadir of his fortunes, Jesus asserts, "Yes, I am a king."

Earlier in John's Gospel, after Jesus fed the five thousand, he withdrew to a mountain by himself when he "realized that they were about to come and take him by force to make him king" (6:15). By any standard we know, that was the moment to admit that he was a king, not now, when his friends are scattered, one of his closest followers has betrayed him, and another has denied him three times. Yet he does not claim that he is a king when he is on top, but rather when he has hit rock bottom. There is something to ponder here.

Jesus, we believe, is *the* revelation of who God is and what God values. That revelation reaches its climax in the crucifixion and resurrection of Jesus. So Jesus' claim of kingship at this nadir of his earthly power says something about God as well as about Jesus. Yes, for God, appearance and reality are topsy-turvy. The ones with power—Annas and Caiaphas, Herod, Pilate—have nothing that God holds dear or that would make them kings in God's eyes, whereas the one with no power, the one who has been handed over to the powerful ones, has what God holds dear. Indeed, Christian artists have always known that Jesus dying on the cross as a common criminal is God's version of what a king is and should be. This beaten, bruised young man, torn and bleeding, crowned with thorns, horribly racked by thirst and pain, is the Savior of the world, the long-awaited Messiah, God's king.

## GETTING PAST OUR PRESUPPOSITIONS AND PREJUDICES

Pondering the paradox of the scene at Pilate's palace should shake up some of our deeply ingrained presuppositions and prejudices, but only if we let the message of the scene sink in. We are, after all, conditioned by our culture to judge by appearances. Why else are we so shocked by revelations of child abuse among the affluent and almost take it for granted among the poor? Why else do we assume that the children of the well-to-do will be academically bright, while those of the poor and of minorities will be academically slow? Crime in run-down neighborhoods of our inner cities is expected; it is news when it occurs in upper-class neighborhoods. The shock value of the parable of the good Samaritan (Luke 10:25–37) rests on the assumptions and prejudices of Jesus' audience. The priest and the Levite would be expected to act charitably toward the wounded man. No one in Jesus' audience would expect such behavior from a despised Samaritan. For an audience today, we would have to change the Samaritan into a member of the most despised and disregarded group we know.

Is it not true that we are genuinely surprised by kindness and charity shown to us by someone of a different cultural or social background? Much in our culture teaches us to esteem and expect more of well-educated, well-dressed, well-heeled people. We look up to those who have power and esteem. (I am rather amazed at the change in attitude that comes over people when they hear that I was provincial of the Jesuits, as though having had that job automatically makes me a better person.) We do tend to judge by appearances. We do not, from our culture, imbibe God's values. We need to let the horror of the Crucifixion shock us into the realization that we do not judge as God does.

In his inimitable style, Frederick Buechner contrasts appearances and reality from the point of view of the Gospels in his book *Telling the Truth*:

> In the world of the fairy tale, the wicked sisters are dressed as if for a Palm Beach wedding, and in the world of the Gospel it is the killjoys, the phonies, the nitpickers, the holier-than-thous, the loveless and cheerless and irrelevant who more often than not wear the fancy clothes and go riding around in sleek little European jobs marked Pharisee, Corps Diplomatique, Legislature, Clergy. It is the ravening wolves who wear sheep's clothing. And the good ones, the potentially good anyway, the ones who stand a chance of being saved by God because they know they don't stand a chance of being saved by anybody else? They go around looking like the town whore, the village drunk, the crook from the IRS, because that is who they are. . . .
>
> And as for king of the kingdom himself, whoever would recognize him? He has no form or comeliness. . . . He smells of mortality. We have romanticized his raggedness so long that we can catch echoes only of

> the way it must have scandalized his time in the horri-
> fied question of the Baptist's disciples. "Are *you* he who
> is to come?" [Matthew 11:3]; in Pilate's "Are you the
> king of the Jews?" (Matthew 27:11).

In a memorable homily to the novices of the New England Province of the Society of Jesus, the late David Donovan, SJ, made the following point: To become a member of most organizations, one has to have some positive quality. To become a member of Mensa, a person must prove that his or her IQ is at or above the ninety-eighth percentile on a standardized intelligence test. To get into a university, one needs a diploma or a GED. To become a member of the American Medical Association, one must be a medical student, a resident physician, or a physician who has earned a medical degree. Donovan noted that it does not work this way with Alcoholics Anonymous. To become a member of AA, one need only stand up in a meeting and say, "I'm Joe, and I'm an alcoholic."

Many people do not get the help they need because they are ashamed to make this statement. Appearances get in the way of reality. The reality is that most people react with admiration when someone admits the truth that will set him or her free. Donovan then went on to note that the requirement for membership in the Christian church is similar to that of AA. One need only say, "I'm Joe, and I'm a sinner in need of salvation." Again, many find it difficult to admit their reality and so hide behind appearances, thus depriving themselves of saving grace, freedom, and a path to true happiness.

The parable of the prodigal son illustrates God's view of reality. The father embraces with love and happiness the son who admits that he is a sinner in need of forgiveness. To enter into a more intimate relationship with God, we need no other qualification than the willingness to admit the truth about ourselves. But because of our conditioning, we find it quite difficult to admit the truth and thus move toward freedom and joy, the kind of freedom and joy described by Gerard Manley Hopkins at the end of his poem "That Nature Is a Heraclitean Fire and of the Comfort of the Resurrection":

> In a flash, at a trumpet crash,
> I am all at once what Christ is, since he was what I
>     am, and
> This Jack, joke, poor potsherd, patch, matchwood,
>     immortal diamond,
>     Is immortal diamond.

In following Jesus as disciples, we are tripped up by our presuppositions and prejudices, just as the disciples were. In Mark's Gospel, three times Jesus predicts his imminent crucifixion and death, and each time the disciples miss the message because they are blinded by their own assumptions about what kind of Messiah will come. After the first prediction, Peter in horror takes Jesus aside and begins to rebuke him (8:31–33). After the second, the disciples get into an argument as to which of them is the greatest (9:30–37). After the third, James and John approach Jesus and ask to sit at his right and left in his kingdom. When the other disciples hear of this, they become indignant (10:32–45). Those of us who want to become Jesus' disciples can be blinded just as easily.

In Fyodor Dostoevsky's *The Brothers Karamazov*, Ivan tells the story of the Grand Inquisitor, in which Jesus is once again killed, but this time by the leaders of the Catholic Church in Spain at the time of the Inquisition. If Jesus were to reappear in our midst, would he fare any better than he did in Roman-occupied Palestine? We have some evidence of how he would be treated in the way that those who follow him unreservedly are treated. The kind of honesty and willingness to face reality that got Jesus killed can infect those who get close to him now and get them killed. Witness Archbishop Oscar Romero of El Salvador. Witness the thousands of catechists in Central and South America who have been killed because they preached the gospel. Witness the Jesuits at the University of Central America, in El Salvador, who were slaughtered along with their cook and her daughter because they told the truth. These and many other cruel murders testify to the fact that our "Christian" world still judges reality differently than God does.

Moreover, we may resist getting close to Jesus because we fear the consequences for our lifestyle. In a previous meditation, we pondered the story of the rich young man, whose attachment to his great wealth keeps him from following Jesus. He goes away grieving. The sad aspect of the story is that the young man loses what he most wants because of the illusion that he cannot do without his wealth. The reality is that his deepest happiness lies in following his heart's desire, which is to be with Jesus. Again we see that appearances get in the way of seeing reality.

We come back to Jesus facing Pilate and his own death by crucifixion. In this dark hour, Jesus reveals what is at the heart of reality. It is a self-sacrificing God, a God who embraces what is most antithetical to him—namely, death and evil—and makes them part of who he is. After this dark hour, anyone who contemplates Jesus sees God in a human body with the wounds of the Crucifixion in his hands, feet, and side. As he stood before Pilate and hung on the cross at Golgotha, Jesus would by appearances seem to be a total failure; it appeared that he had not brought about the conversion of his people. Indeed, if this "worm and no man" was the Messiah, then God had perpetrated a cruel hoax on his people. Lying, cowardly kowtowing to Roman authority, cruelty, and naked power had prevailed. On the cross, Jesus was mocked and ridiculed; and if he is God, then God was mocked and ridiculed. Evil seems to have triumphed. It is hard to imagine anything more antithetical to God than the unspeakable horrors that are visited upon this innocent human being.

Yet the reality is that Jesus is a king; the Jesus so horribly tortured is God incarnate, "the power of God and the wisdom of God" (1 Corinthians 1:24). The powers of darkness and the evil that lurks in the hearts of human beings have their day and seem to win. But Jesus, the power and wisdom of God, lets them have their way, embraces what they have to do, and, in the face of all that overpowering evil, can say, precisely because of his oneness with God, "Father, forgive them; for they do not know what they are doing" (Luke 23:34).

It will pay to reflect over and over again on this mystery of Jesus, the suffering king. In creation, God produces what is not God—namely, our universe. God could not be Creator without the existence of the universe. God, however, does not create out of necessity, but because of overflowing love. With the Crucifixion, this love surpasses all human grasp, because now God bears in human flesh the results of appalling evil. To be the Christ he now is, these wounds are necessary. The appearances of powerlessness, of criminality, of absolute weakness are now the reality of God. As Paul says, "For the message about the cross is foolishness to those who are perishing, but to us who are being saved it is the power of God" (1 Corinthians 1:18).

If we pay attention to the deepest desires of our hearts, we know that only union with God will satisfy us. But union with God leads us to see reality in a new way, requiring a reevaluation of what is real and what is appearance.

In "God's Grandeur," Hopkins catches the difference between appearance and reality for those who believe in the kingship of the broken Jesus.

The world is charged with the grandeur of God.
    It will flame out, like shining from shook foil;
    It gathers to a greatness, like the ooze of oil
Crushed. Why do men then now not reck his rod?
Generations have trod, have trod, have trod;
    And all is seared with trade; bleared, smeared with
        toil;
    And wears man's smudge and shares man's smell:
        the soil
Is bare now, nor can foot feel, being shod.

And for all this, nature is never spent;
    There lives the dearest freshness deep down
        things;
And though the last lights off the black West went
    Oh, morning, at the brown brink eastward,
        springs—
Because the Holy Ghost over the bent
    World broods with warm breast and with ah!
        bright wings.

## ❖ 10 ❖

# MYSTICISM IN HELL

The word *mystic* usually conjures up images of nuns wrapped in voluminous, flowing gowns swooning in ecstasy, or fierce ascetics of the desert fighting off the devil's allures. Mystics are associated with cloisters, with vows of poverty and chastity, and with long hours of prayer in monastery cells and chapels.

What are we to make, then, of Etty Hillesum, the Dutch Jewish woman who died at Auschwitz on November 30, 1943? In her diaries, published under the title *An Interrupted Life*, she says, knowing full well that arrest and transport await her: "Once you have begun to walk with God, you need only keep on walking with Him and all of life becomes one long stroll— such a marvelous feeling. . . . I hate nobody. I am not embittered. And once the love of mankind has germinated in you, it will grow without measure." This entry and others witness to a union with God that can only be called mystical.

Yet Hillesum was no cloistered virgin. Her first entry says: "I am accomplished in bed, just about seasoned enough I should think to be counted among the better lovers, and love does indeed suit me to perfection, and yet it remains a mere trifle, set apart from what is truly essential, and deep inside me something is still locked away." Her diaries attest to a somewhat bohemian lifestyle far from monastic quiet. And, of course, the menace of the Nazi occupiers permeates the atmosphere. Those of us who out of necessity have to find God in the hurly-burly of an active lifestyle and in less-than-ideal personal circumstances may find encouragement in reflecting on Hillesum's diaries.

## A GROWING UNION WITH GOD

Etty Hillesum was born on January 15, 1914, one of three rather brilliant children of the turbulent marriage between a Dutch Jewish schoolteacher and headmaster and a Russian Jewish woman. After leaving her father's school in 1932, Hillesum took her first degree, in law, at the University of Amsterdam and then enrolled in the Department of Slavic Languages. Her diaries indicate that she paid some of her living expenses by tutoring in Russian. We do not know much of her life before Sunday, March 9, 1941, when she made her first diary entry. From the diaries, we learn that her life revolved around two circles of people, one the group of five with whom she lived, the other a group of followers of a somewhat enigmatic and mesmerizing German Jew named Julius Spier.

The group of five was headed by a sixty-two-year-old widower, Han Wegerif, who had invited Hillesum in as a sort of housekeeper. She soon became his lover. Hillesum met Spier in January 1941, it seems, and also became his patient in a rather strange psychotherapy that included wrestling. After a few sessions, she became his confidant and then his lover. Psychologists would have a field day analyzing Hillesum's transference and Spier's countertransference. Yet through this relationship, Hillesum found God. After Spier died, in September 1942, Hillesum addressed him in her diary: "You taught me to speak the name of God without embarrassment. You were the mediator between God and me, and now you, the mediator, have gone, and my path leads straight to God. It is right that it should be so. And I shall be the mediator for any other soul I can reach."

Whatever else we can say about the therapeutic relationship between Hillesum and Spier—and Hillesum was not blind to Spier's weaknesses—he was the catalyst for a remarkable transformation in her. In the course of the year and a half recorded in her diaries, Hillesum developed from a young woman controlled by her moods and fears to a spiritually mature person who could fairly be described as a mystic in the hell created by the Nazis in occupied Europe. How did this transformation come about?

What strikes a reader immediately is her fierce candor about herself and her situation and her strong desire to be true to her God. In November 1941, she noted that something had pulled her back to her roots. As she cycled home the night before, she babbled something like this:

> God, take me by Your hand, I shall follow You dutifully, and not resist too much. I shall evade none of the tempests life has in store for me, I shall try to face it all as best I can. But now and then grant me a short respite. I shall never again assume, in my innocence, that any peace that comes my way will be eternal. I shall accept all the inevitable tumult and struggle. I delight in warmth and security, but I shall not rebel if I have to suffer cold, should You so decree. I shall follow wherever Your hand leads me and shall try not to be afraid. I shall try to spread some of my warmth, of my genuine love for others, wherever I go. But we shouldn't boast of our love for others. We cannot be sure that it really exists. I don't want to be anything special, I only want to try to be true to that in me which seeks to fulfill its promise. I sometimes imagine that I long for the seclusion of a nunnery. But I know that I must seek You among people, out in the world.

Along with the candor about herself, she seems to have developed a willingness to speak honestly to God. In April 1942, responding to unflattering comments made about her, she wrote:

I am still assailed far too much by words like these. I prayed early this morning, "Lord, free me from all these petty vanities. They take up too much of my inner life, and I know only too well that other things matter much more than being thought nice and charming by one's fellows." What I mean is, that sort of thing mustn't take up too much of your time and imagination. For then you get carried away with: "What a nice person I am, what fun I am, how much everyone must like me."

By the end of April, her spiritual regimen of candor with herself and God led to this assertion:

Instead of living an accidental life, you feel deep down that you have grown mature enough to accept your "destiny." . . .

And that is the great change of the last year. I don't have to mess about with my thoughts anymore or tinker with my life, for an organic process is at work. Something in me is growing, and every time I look inside, something fresh has appeared and all I have to do is to accept it, to take it upon myself, to bear it forward, and to let it flourish.

Prayer also seems to have been a part of her deepening relationship with God. On May 18, 1942, she wrote about the growing threat and terror all around her and then said, "I draw prayer round me like a dark protective wall, withdraw inside it as one might into a convent cell and then step outside again, calmer and stronger and more collected again."

On June 20, she spoke of seeing more and more signs barring Jews from most paths and open country. Then she added:

> But above the one narrow path still left to us stretches the sky, intact. They can't do anything to us, they really can't. They can harass us, they can rob us of our material goods, of our freedom of movement, but we ourselves forfeit our greatest assets by our misguided compliance. By our feelings of being persecuted, humiliated, and oppressed. By our own hatred. . . . We may of course be sad and depressed by what has been done to us; that is only human and understandable. However: our greatest injury is one we inflict upon ourselves. I find life beautiful, and I feel free. The sky within me is as wide as the one stretching above my head. I believe in God and I believe in man, and I say so without embarrassment. Life is hard, but that is no bad thing. . . . True peace will come only when every individual finds peace within himself; when we have all vanquished and transformed our hatred for our fellow human beings of whatever race—even into love one day, although perhaps that is asking too much. It is, however, the only solution. I am a happy person and I hold life dear indeed, in this year of Our Lord 1942, the umpteenth year of the war.

As the diaries come to an end, one senses an ever-deepening conviction in her that no matter what happens—and she never shuts her eyes to the horrible fate in store for her and all Jews—God will sustain her. Indeed, she becomes more and more convinced that her mission in life is to accept into her heart the sufferings of others and not to respond with bitterness. When she does quaver before the enormity she faces, she pours out her heart to her God and finds peace. For example, here is a Sunday morning prayer in July 1942:

> Dear God, these are anxious times. Tonight for the first time I lay in the dark with burning eyes as scene after scene of human suffering passed before me. I shall promise You one thing, God, just one very small thing: I shall never burden my today with cares about my tomorrow, although that takes some practice. Each day is sufficient unto itself. I shall try to help You, God, to stop my strength ebbing away, though I cannot vouch for it in advance. But one thing is becoming increasingly clear to me: that You cannot help us, that we must help You to help ourselves. And that is all we can manage these days and also all that really matters: that we safeguard that little piece of You, God, in ourselves. And perhaps in others as well. . . . No one is in their clutches who is in Your arms. I am beginning to feel a little more peaceful, God, thanks to this conversation.

These last words speak volumes about how Hillesum developed her relationship with God and point the way any one of us can take—namely, to pour out our hearts to God.

Hillesum's conversations with God were not only about painful matters. Later on in that same prayer, she recalls the jasmine tree behind her house that was destroyed by storms, and then goes on to say to God:

> But somewhere inside me the jasmine continues to blossom undisturbed, just as profusely and delicately as ever it did. And it spreads its scent round the House in which You dwell, oh God. You can see, I look after You, I bring You not only my tears and my forebodings on this stormy, gray Sunday morning, I even bring You scented jasmine. And I shall bring You all the flowers I shall meet on my way, and truly there are many of those. I shall try to make You at home always. Even if I should be locked up in a narrow cell and a cloud should drift past my small barred window, then I shall bring You that cloud, oh God, while there is still the strength in me to do so. I cannot promise You anything for tomorrow, but my intentions are good, You can see.

Because of her inner transformation, she desired to become "a center of peace" in the "madhouse" that was the Jewish Council, where she worked for a couple of weeks, and then the "thinking heart" of Westerbork camp. She was convinced that the world's only hope was for human beings to accept life, with all its bitterness and suffering, lovingly. And she conceived her "apostolate" in this way:

> How great are the needs of Your creatures on this earth, oh God. They sit there, talking quietly and quite unsuspecting, and suddenly their need erupts in all its nakedness. Then, there they are, bundles of human misery, desperate and unable to face life. And that's when my task begins. It is not enough simply to proclaim You, God, to commend You to the hearts of others. One must also clear the path toward You in them, God, and to do that one has to be a keen judge of the human soul. . . . I embark on a slow voyage of exploration with everyone who comes to me. And I thank You for the great gift of being able to read people. Sometimes they seem to me like houses with open doors. . . . And every one must be turned into a dwelling dedicated to You, oh God. And I promise You, yes, I promise that I shall try to find a dwelling and a refuge for You in as many houses as possible.

Later that month, she wrote again of her desires:

> With a sharp pang, all of suffering mankind's nocturnal distress and loneliness passes now through my

small heart. What shall I be taking upon myself this winter?

"One day, I would love to travel through all the world, oh God; I feel drawn right across all frontiers and feel a bond with all Your warring creatures." And I would like to proclaim that bond in a small, still voice but also compellingly and without pause. But first I must be present on every battlefront and at the center of all human suffering.

Her diaries end with these words: "We should be willing to act as a balm for all wounds." Apparently, Hillesum was willing.

These diaries give eloquent testimony that even in the hell of the Final Solution, God was not absent, that relating to God openly and candidly can transform a person dramatically, and that we do not need to be very "pious" or even "religious," in the ordinary sense of the terms, to engage in a relationship with God. God, it seems, is ready to engage in a relationship with us whenever we want to begin. We do not even have to "get our act together" before we can begin to relate to God. Finally, Etty Hillesum's diaries show us that those who help us on the way to God may be people we least expect.

## ❖ 11 ❖

# THE INVENTIVENESS OF GOD

Do you remember how you reacted when you first heard that heaven would consist of the beatific vision? "What's that?" you might have said in your head, if not out loud. When it was explained that the beatific vision meant looking at and enjoying God for all eternity, did you wonder if you'd be bored, if there would be something else to do? Being polite before God, if you did have such thoughts, you were probably like me and kept them to yourself. After all, heaven is a long way off, and there are still a lot of interesting things to do and see here on earth. The beatific vision could take care of itself, whatever it might mean.

I have claimed that our deepest desire is for union with God. Often, people find prayer—which aims for union with God—boring. It seems paradoxical that our deepest desire may lead to boredom. Does it?

A couple of years ago, I had an insight that made the thought of heaven a lot more intriguing than the idea of gawking at a throne forever. I had spent the month of January at Eastern Point Retreat House, in Gloucester, Massachusetts, directing people on retreat. Every day, without exception, at least five or six of the thirty-day retreatants could be found in the dining room, looking out to sea through the picture windows for over an hour as the sky brightened and the sun rose. Since some of them talked to me each day about their prayer, I found out that they were never bored by this activity. Each day brought something new. The cloud pattern varied endlessly and affected how the light of the sun was reflected. Some days, the sun had to break through a low-lying bank of fog; other days, the sun itself never appeared, but still the darkness dissipated. The light on the water also varied, depending on the tide, the direction of the wind, the temperature, and the cloud pattern. Each day also brought new experiences of God as they watched the sun rise.

Gloucester teems with bird life. Just the gulls alone are worth the price of admission. They come in various shades of gray, white, and black and seem to revel in soaring with the wind, or sometimes against it, so that they seem motionless. At times, they congregate by the hundreds on the iced-over pond, facing in one direction for long periods of time. Sandpipers often do the same thing on one leg, droves of them all facing in the same direction. They even hop on the one leg. It seems as if they are playing a game, and the first to use two legs loses. Both the pond and the cove abound with ducks of all varieties, and the closer you look, the more variegated are their colors. Some of the greens you can see only in a certain light and up close. Back in the city, I noticed a similar phenomenon in an ordinary pigeon; it turned in the sunlight, and just for a moment I saw a beautiful greenish blue in its neck feathers.

I enjoy watching the cormorants dive under the water and waiting for them to surface, and realizing that the ones who emerge are the same ones who dove minutes before. Then there are the swans, like little boats in the water. The original two at Eastern Point now seem to have grown to at least ten. In the last two days of January, I counted eight sailing serenely in Brace's Cove, and later two more at Rocky Neck. They were so stately and lovely to look at, but I also wanted to see them fly and land. Finally, I saw one of them come in for a landing and was surprised at how graceful it was.

Of course, there are also land birds around, not as many as in summer, but still an amazing number. You hear them more often than you see them. The caws of the crows are everywhere. One sound intrigued me for days because I could not determine its source. Whenever I heard it, I saw only crows nearby, and I thought it was too melodious to come from them. But sure enough, one day I heard the sound and saw it coming from a crow. Even they have a lovely sound at times.

Twice during the month, I caught sight of seals on the rocks in the cove. The first time, I saw a rather little one, and relatively far away, so that even the binoculars did not give much of a look. But on the last day of the thirty-day retreat, I saw a large seal on a rock fairly close by. The tide was coming in and gradually washing over more and more of the rock. The seal raised its head and tail as each wave moved over the rock, then finally gave up its perch and slid into the sea.

Whenever someone contemplates making a thirty-day retreat for the first time, he or she wonders how the time will pass. "Will I be bored?" "How many books should I bring?" "How can I ever spend that much time in prayer?" These are some of the questions that run through the minds of prospective retreatants—not unlike the kinds of questions we might ask about heaven, if we ever give heaven a thought. During that January, I found that the retreatants were bored only when they became resistant to God's presence and closeness. For the most part, they were eager to spend time in prayer, because the periods of prayer were so interesting. They found that God was not boring as company, and they did not seem boring to God.

## The Endless Variety of Creation

I have now directed perhaps two hundred people on thirty-day retreats, and many more than that on eight-day retreats. As a director, I see each person each day of the retreat to talk about what happened in his or her prayer during the previous day. Not only am I not bored, but I also find myself eager to listen to each new person. In the case of experiences of the relationship with God, it is clearly not true that "when you've seen one, you've seen them all." Part of my motivation for being a spiritual director springs from the endless variety of people's experiences of God. When I listen to them, I learn more about God.

Let me return to the insight I referred to in the opening paragraphs of the meditation. One day it dawned on me that God's creation has intrigued human beings since the beginning of time. We have never tired of looking at, listening to, smelling, touching, testing, trying to figure out, trying to understand, or trying to control the created universe. Curiosity impels a child to try to make sense of his or her world; the same curiosity impels an astronomer to spend days at a telescope or poring over photos in order to understand the universe. For human beings, there are always new things to discover, to learn, to sense.

The mystery writer Jane Langton, in her novel *Good and Dead*, notes that the minister Joe Bold has always been intrigued by the details around him. In adulthood, he

> learned that these airy manifestations were metaphors, mystical pedagogical remarks by God, who never stopped talking in a language composed of the droplets in a cloud or the sap running up a tree, or the willful behavior of the elements of a dividing cell. It was a garrulous communication that never ceased, a gabble of molecules, a continuous proclamation by cobblestones and the bark of trees, by constellations of stars and by cracks in the sidewalk, an endless monologue of visual splendors.

Think of how you can listen to an intriguing piece of music or read a novel or poem over and over again and discover new wrinkles each time. These are human creations, and the human creator is only a pale image of the Creator of the universe. The poet Brendan Galvin said in an interview, "Some writers come to feel that the reason the world exists is so that we can write about it." We can paraphrase him, perhaps, by saying that the reason the world exists is so that we can live in it, and in the living become enthralled not only by the world but by its Creator and ours. We would need an eternity to enjoy the inventiveness, the playfulness and seriousness, the simplicity and complexity of our God. Heaven, whatever it is, will not be boring.

Of course, there's no need to rush it, is there?

Part 3

# ACTIONS

# DOES GOD NEED US?

The question in the title of this meditation seems absurd. For the believer, God is absolutely self-sufficient. The triune community is perfect and needs no one and nothing else. Indeed, if God needed anyone or anything else, God would not be God. So the first answer to the question, does God need us? has to be an emphatic no. God creates the universe and us not out of need, but because of overflowing love. As Sebastian Moore notes in *Let This Mind Be in You*, our desire for someone or something is aroused by its existing beauty, but God's desire for a universe and for us brings both into existence.

This doctrine has often been misused to make people feel useless before God. I want to reflect with you in this meditation in such a way that we can give a positive, and orthodox, answer to the question of the title.

## How We Are Needed

If God, freely and out of love, wants to be Creator of the universe, what is needed? Obviously, God must will the existence of the universe. If God wants to have a universe where human beings can be invited into the community life of the Trinity, then people who can receive the invitation and respond to it are necessary. Thus, there is a real sense in which God "needs" the universe and the persons in it, but only because God freely decides to become the Creator of the universe and to invite people into the community life of the Trinity.

We can take the argument a step further. The kingdom of God that Jesus preached can be understood as God's intention for the universe—namely, that it be a place where all men and women live in communion with the Trinity and thus in harmony with one another and the rest of the universe. God wants the whole human race to become friends with God. But friendship cannot be coerced; human beings must freely choose to accept God's invitation. Thus, God needs people who will hear the word and live it out. God "needs" hearers and doers of the word in order to be who he wants to be for us.

Recently, I was reflecting on the confession of Peter at Caesarea Philippi. The scene is central to the synoptic Gospels (Matthew, Mark, and Luke). After it, the die seems cast as far as Jesus is concerned: he turns his face resolutely toward Jerusalem and also begins earnestly teaching his disciples what his mission will be, three times predicting his passion and death. In the scene, Jesus asks the disciples, "Who do people say that I am?" When they tell him what people are saying, he says, "But who do you say that I am?" Peter answers for all, "You are the Messiah" (see Mark 8:27–30). Often enough when we contemplate this scene, we focus on who Jesus is for us, and rightly so. But it is also possible to look at the scene from Jesus' point of view. Could it not be that Jesus needs the disciples' response in order to clarify his own growing sense of his identity and destiny? Let us ponder this possibility for a few moments.

How does anyone come to know who he or she is and what lifework he or she will do? Certainly part of the answer comes from internal processes. I reflect on my desires, hopes, and dreams. In prayer, I may ask God to help me know how I should best live out my life. I notice my attractions, the kinds of people and things that fire my imagination. Mentally, I try on roles and professions. I may even apprentice myself for a time to a few possible lifeworks. But unless I am a megalomaniac or a pure dreamer, I cannot really know my identity and my mission without dialogue with others. For example, in an extended retreat by myself, I may come to the clear decision that I should become a Jesuit. But before I can really know that this discernment is correct—that it is, as Ignatius of Loyola would say, confirmed— I must be accepted by the Society of Jesus and then must submit myself to the long process of becoming a Jesuit through interaction with other Jesuits in formation.

I like to speculate that for Jesus, this dialogue with the disciples was part of his coming to terms with his role in life and his destiny as Messiah. Jesus, like any human being, could not establish his identity without the help of others. This scene, looked at in this way, shows that Jesus needs the response of Peter to confirm his own sense of mission.

Obviously, Jesus is not now discerning who he is and what his mission is to be, so he does not need our response in order to confirm his identity. But is there a way in which our recognition of Jesus as Savior and dearest friend affects Jesus and his mission? First, suppose that no one now living recognized Jesus as Savior and Messiah. Then, in effect, he would not be Savior for anyone. Moreover, there would be no one who related meaningfully to Jesus and thus made him present in the world; there would be no human sacramental signs of Jesus. Finally, even if Jesus is, by his very being as God and human, intimately related to our world and to all people as Savior and Redeemer, it would be almost impossible for anyone to know of this reality. For all practical purposes, Jesus would be absent from the world people know, and he would have no relevance for us.

In other words, without people who recognize and proclaim Jesus for who he is and wants to be, Jesus would not be who he wants to be in this world. Thus, Jesus must still be interested in our responses to the question, who do you say I am? Jesus still needs people who recognize him and believe in him in order to fulfill his mission to our world.

Let's continue along this line of reflection. Wherever we live and work, we believe, Jesus is present as Savior and Redeemer, as brother of every human being we meet. But who makes his presence palpable? Is it not the person who believes in and loves Jesus? Since the Resurrection, Jesus has needed the hands of Christians to reach out to touch with love and sympathy those who are suffering, has needed the compassionate eyes of Christians to show his compassion, has needed the hearts of Christians to demonstrate his love for people whom these Christians meet. In front of Christ the King Church in San Diego, there is a statue of Christ with no hands. This illustrates that Jesus needs the hands of his followers now. Those who believe in and love Jesus are changed by the quality of that relationship; they act differently than they would if they did not believe in and love Jesus.

A story may illustrate my meaning. In an article in the *Atlantic* in 1964, the writer Garson Kanin recounted his visits to Felix Frankfurter, the associate justice of the Supreme Court. One day, Frankfurter said:

> I have had a serious experience here. . . . You saw that nurse who went out a while ago? The tall, pretty, blond one? Audrée? We've been spending many hours here together, and I've had an opportunity to find out a great deal about her life. She is a devout Catholic. Look here. I have spent a good deal of energy attempting to avoid prejudice. But the dogma of the Catholic Church, or

of any other denomination for that matter, has always put me off. Now this girl, this Audrée—I have never known generosity of such quality, or such rare kindness. Oh yes, far, far beyond duty. Overwhelming courtesy. And I have been asking questions, delving into the matter, trying to discover the wellspring of such superior behavior. Do you know what it turns out to be? Can you guess? Simply this—a practical application of her Catholicism. I've never known anyone who practiced a religion, whose everyday life is based upon a religion as much as this girl's is.

Audrée may never have known the impact her lived faith had, but she made Jesus a palpable presence in that hospital. She supplied the hands Jesus needed there. So a real relationship with Jesus has an impact even when the person who has that relationship does not mention Jesus. I venture to say that Jesus needs people like Audrée in order to be who he wants to be for people like Felix Frankfurter.

Of course, those who believe in and love Jesus can also, when it is appropriate, speak openly of the one whom they love. We say that we believe in the resurrection of Jesus. That means, at least, that Jesus can be experienced as a real, comforting presence to those who suffer and grieve. Does it not also mean that our loved ones who have died in Christ can be experienced as somehow alive in Christ? The risen Jesus needs friends who have experienced his reality in their lives to spread the word so that others may also open their hearts to experience his reality in this world. It is only with difficulty that Jesus can be the consoler he wants to be if we who believe in him and experience him as our consoler and friend do not witness to him.

Finally, if God can be found in all things, as Ignatian spirituality proposes, then those of us who take this spirituality seriously are "needed" by God to discover his presence in the mundane details of our own lives. If we can do that for ourselves, then perhaps we will be more able to help others discover "the dearest freshness deep down things," as Gerard Manley Hopkins puts it. God needs people who, like Hopkins, can point to the signs of hope and love in a world that often seems bereft of both and of God.

In the letter to the Romans, Paul touches on our topic when he says:

> For there is no distinction between Jew and Greek; the same Lord is Lord of all and is generous to all who call on him. For, "Everyone who calls on the name of the Lord shall be saved."
>
> But how are they to call on one in whom they have not believed? And how are they to believe in one of whom they have never heard? And how are they to hear without someone to proclaim him? And how are they

> to proclaim him unless they are sent? As it is written,
> "How beautiful are the feet of those who bring good
> news!" (10:12–15)

Out of love, not necessity, God is now in the position of depending on us for what he hopes for the world. We are important to, indeed needed by, God. What divine condescension! What great love!

## ❖ 13 ❖

# WHAT ROLE DO WE PLAY IN THE KINGDOM OF GOD?

Christians often talk about building up the kingdom of God. But only God builds up the kingdom. The kingdom of God can be understood as God's one action, an action whose intention is to create an environment where all people can enter into God's own community life. We do not build up the kingdom of God; rather, we discover it insofar as we discern how to align our actions with the one action of God. We discover it, in other words, when we live as brothers and sisters with the intent of not excluding any person in principle from our community, and when we create structures that make the universal community of all people more possible.

In a session of spiritual direction, I had an insight about another role we play in the discovery of God's kingdom.

Christians believe that God is both transcendent and immanent in this world. That is, we believe that at every moment of the world's existence, God is mysteriously acting to achieve the one intention for the world. Ignatian spirituality speaks of finding God in all things, which assumes that God is "in all things" in some mysterious way. Thus, in any situation, God is present and active—and therefore, to be found.

But suppose that no one was aware of God's presence. Is God then present in all things? I am reminded of the question, does a tree falling in the woods make a noise if there is no one there to hear it? An example may help. A family is gathered around a dying father in a hospital room. Christians believe that God is present there in some mysterious way. But none of those present are aware of or expecting God's presence. As the family watches silently and mourns, each person experiences a variety of emotions, from anguish and despair to a strange sense of peace. While the father slips further into a coma, some embrace, one or two hold his hand, and all sense that, painful as it is, it is good to be here. Afterward, if they talk about the experience with one another, they may speak of the together-ness and peace they felt. But they probably will not pay much attention to it, and it will soon pass out of memory. God, we might say, has been actively present in this sad situation, but no one noticed. One result of not noticing might well be a return to their normal relationships, which are mostly distant and even acrimonious. A chance for reconciliation and deeper communion has been lost for lack of awareness. Yet in those moments as their father was dying, they experienced the kingdom of God, God's action inviting them to consciously become a community in union with the Trinity.

Now let's introduce into the same scene a family member who is alert to the presence of God in our world. She, too, is grieving the impending loss of her father, but she also prays silently, asking God to take care of him and the family. She notices the change of mood in the room as the family members begin to comfort one another and say good-bye to their father. She feels closer to all of them herself, even to the two brothers from whom she has been estranged. Her heart fills with gratitude to God as she recognizes the divine hand at work in the room. Later, she rather shyly tells her brothers and sisters of her experience in the hospital room. They respond in kind, each recounting his or her own reactions during their father's dying moments. As they talk, they become aware of a deeper bond between them and have a sense that their father is still with them, just as, they now believe, God is with them.

What role do we Christians have in God's one action, which is the kingdom of God? One role, at least, is to become aware of God's action in our daily lives and to witness to it. In other words, God needs us not so much to bring about his kingdom as to notice its presence in our midst. Wherever in our world people who should be enemies become friends; wherever injured people forgive those who have injured them; wherever love and care for another overcome fear of the other; wherever the hungry are fed, the thirsty given a cup of water, the naked clothed, the homeless housed, and prisoners visited—wherever, in other words, a community that is in principle inclusive exists—the kingdom of God is present there, and it is moving forward (see Matthew 25:31–46). But God's active presence will be missed if no one notices it or witnesses to it. Of course, we can notice God's active presence only if we are on the alert for it, if we believe in and expect that God will be actively present to our lives. The two disciples on the road to Emmaus did not expect to meet the living Jesus on their journey. As a result, even though their hearts were burning as they walked along with the stranger and listened to him, they did not recognize him until much later, at the breaking of the bread (Luke 24:13–32). Our first task, then, is to ask God to help us achieve a practical belief in his active presence in our lives.

Then we must school ourselves to pay attention to our experience in order to discern the touch of God, or what the sociologist Peter Berger calls the "rumor of angels," from all other influences. Every human experience is multidimensional, having physical, biological, psychological, sociological, and cultural influences. But for believers, there is also a religious dimension to every experience, since we believe that at every moment of existence human beings encounter God. Discernment seeks to distinguish, within our experience, what is of God from what is not of God. (We might add here that another influence on our experience is the Evil One. A friend recently noted that our culture is coming around to the belief that God is not dead, but we have not yet come to believe in the existence of the devil, in spite of the massive evidence in our time of unparalleled evil.) God needs people who take the time to notice the divine action in the world. That is, God needs people who believe in a practical way in God's active presence in this world and take the steps to discover it through prayer, paying attention to their experience, and discernment. To become such practical believers, many Christians in our day have returned to the ancient practice of consulting a spiritual director regularly.

Finally, having discerned the active presence of God in the events of our daily lives, we need to be willing to witness to what we have seen and heard: "We declare to you what was from the beginning, what we have heard, what we have seen with our eyes, what we have looked at and touched with our hands, concerning the word of life" (1 John 1:1). We do not have to become a preacher, like the writer of the first letter of John. But each of us who notices the active presence of God can learn ways of pointing to that presence. Such pointing will be tentative, to be sure, because we are fallible human beings. Perhaps all we need to do is take the chance of talking about our experience.

At a meeting of Jesuits, I felt close to tears of gratitude at the way the discussion was moving from fractiousness and desolation toward reconciliation, real dialogue, and future planning. I silently thanked God. Normally I do not mention such experiences in public, but this time I did. I told the group what

I had experienced and that I believed we had experienced the active presence of God. No one laughed or asked me to defend my statement. I presumed that others, too, felt the finger of God in the proceedings.

A final word on our role in the kingdom of God: Even though we do not build up the kingdom of God, it would not be attained at all if no one cooperated with God's intention of forming a community of people who share in God's own community life. In other words, we cannot discover or discern God's kingdom theoretically, but only in the practice of trying, with God's grace, to attune our actions with God's one action. God is encountered only in the real world, with all its complexity and conflicting claims and influences. If we try to bring our actions into harmony with the one action of God, we are privileged to be co-creators with God—Father, Son, and Holy Spirit—of the one community, which is God's kingdom.

## ❖ 14 ❖

# WHO WILL TELL THE STORY?

In "The Story," the poet Brendan Kennelly imagines a world where the story of Christmas is no longer told.

> The story was not born with Robbie Cox
> Nor with his father
> Nor his father's father
> But farther back than any could remember.
>
> Cox told the story
> Over twelve nights of Christmas.
> It was the story
> Made Christmas real.
> When it was done
> The new year was in,

Made authentic by the story.
The old year was dead,
Buried by the story.
The man endured,
Deepened by the story.

When Cox died
The story died.
Nobody had time
To learn the story.
Christmas shrivelled,
The old year was dust,
The new year nothing special,
So much time to be endured.
The people withered.
This withering hardly troubled them.
The story was a dead crow in a wet field.
An abandoned house, a rag on a bush,
A sick whisper in a dying room,
The shaking gash of an old man's mouth
Breaking like burnt paper
Into black ashes the wind scatters,
People fleeing from famine.
Nobody has ever heard of them.
Nobody will ever speak for them.
I know the emptiness
Spread by the story's death.

This emptiness is in the roads
And in the fields,
In men's eyes and children's voices,
In summer nights when stars
Play like rabbits behind Cox's house,
House of the story
That once lived on lips
Like starlings startled from a tree,
Exploding in a sky of revelation,
Deliberate and free.

In this poem, we can feel the bleakness left behind with the death of the Christmas story. Now try to imagine what our world would be like without the story of God's passionate love for us. Imagine what it might be like for Jews if the story of the Passover were no longer told as something that affects them now. What if they had no stories of how God had intervened in their history to save them because of his predilection for them? Wouldn't life be barren and hopeless indeed, especially after the history of their persecution, which culminated in the last century with the Holocaust? And yet, thank God, each year all over the world at seders during Passover, the story of the way God brought them as a people out of Egypt is told and gives them hope to face the New Year, with its light and darkness. Moreover, the story is told not as a historical fact that is over and done with, but in such a way that it presently affects those who hear it—much like the way Robbie Cox told the story of Christmas. At the seder, the story is told as something that is occurring now, for the people gathered around the festive table.

Faithful Jews gather daily to recall the saving deeds of Yahweh and to praise and thank God. In Herman Wouk's novel *Inside, Outside*, the protagonist describes his bar mitzvah, when he was a boy of thirteen. He then goes on to say:

> The morning after my bar mitzvah, I returned with Pop to the synagogue. What a contrast! Gloomy, silent, all but empty; down in front, Morris Elfenbein and a few old men putting on prayer shawls and phylacteries. . . .
>
> If Pop hadn't made the effort I'd have missed the whole point. Anybody can stage a big bar mitzvah, given a bundle of money and a boy willing to put up with the drills for the sake of the wingding. The backbone of our religion—who knows, perhaps of all religions in this distracted age—is a stubborn handful in a nearly vacant house of worship, carrying it on for just one more working day; out of habit, loyalty, inertia, superstition, sentiment, or possibly true faith; who can be sure which? My father taught me that somber truth. It has stayed with me, so that I still haul myself to synagogues on weekdays, especially when it rains or snows and the minyan looks chancy.

Here the novelist captures the essence of true religion, that somehow or other the story continues to be told, that somehow the experience of God's saving desire and actions is shared in our "distracted age." Without the faithful remnant telling the story and praising God, there would be "emptiness . . . / In men's eyes and children's voices," as Kennelly says, among Jews throughout the world. Thank God that day after day, year after year, there are people for whom the story of God's love affair with the chosen people is alive and palpable, so alive that they are willing to "haul" themselves to the synagogue on week-days, especially on bad days. Thank God, too, that millions of Jews yearly celebrate the story of the night of Passover as a saving event in their present lives. If no one were to tell the story, then God's saving acts would be lost in the dim reaches of history. They would not affect people now, and the world would be a poorer place indeed.

Think of what it would be like for Christians if no one told the story of the birth, life, death, and resurrection of Jesus anymore. No one would hear the story of Zechariah and Elizabeth, the old childless couple who, wonder of wonders, conceive and bear a child who will be the herald of the long-awaited Messiah. We would miss the sense of hope in God's goodness in spite of appearances that this story rouses. No one would hear the simple yet dazzling story of the angel's appearance to the young girl Mary, the hush of the universe as it waits for her answer, and the sigh of relief when she says, "Here am I, the servant of the Lord; let it be with me accord-ing to your word" (Luke 1:38). We would not hear the story of Jesus, the carpenter's son, who has enthralled millions of people down the centuries with his kindness, his strength, his honesty, and his single-minded devotion to God's kingdom and God's people. No one would know that the desire of the everlasting hills, the hope of the ages, the suffering servant has actually already appeared and has surpassed all expectations and prophecies. We would not know that death has lost its sting, that the light has shone in our darkness and the darkness cannot overcome it. We would not know the joy of the Resurrection. We might have experiences of having our hearts burn within us when we meet a stranger on the road, but we would not know what to make of it and would forget it almost as soon as it happened.

Christians need people who will tell the story of Jesus and of their experiences of Jesus so that we can make sense of our own experiences. A dry textbook description of someone who lived and died two thousand years ago will not feed our imaginations and arouse our desires as God wants them fed and aroused. We need people who witness to the Good News, who tell the story as something real and still powerful now. This is the deepest meaning of the haunting phrase in chapter 52 of Isaiah: "How beautiful upon the mountains / are the feet of the messenger who announces peace, / who brings good news, / who announces salvation, / who says to Zion, 'Your God reigns'" (52:7). Without the telling of the story, there would be no Good News, and our world would be a bleak place indeed—and we the sadder.

## Each of Us Is a Teller of the Story

These reflections lead us to the conclusion that each one of us must be a teller of the story, that each one of us is called to be a piece of Good News for those we meet. We are the Robbie Coxes of our neighborhoods, towns, and cities. We have all experienced the power of the story of God's action in our world, of Jesus as our Savior and dearest friend. We need to tell our stories. A living religion is constituted by the shared faith experiences of all those who belong to that religion, not merely by dogmas and rites and buildings, as important as they are. We all have stories of God and Jesus and the Holy Spirit to tell to one another. Admittedly, the storytelling can be overdone. We do not need compulsive talkers who bore us to death with their self-important tales. But we do need to hear the great things that God has done in our midst.

Nor do our stories have to be lengthy descriptions of "religious experiences." They can be simple stories of a good deed done by a despised Samaritan. They can use the homely metaphor of dough rising because of yeast. Here's a little story I once heard in a homily: A Jesuit priest working in a parish in a neighborhood of mixed new immigrants in Boston was asked at Christmastime by a Buddhist woman whether she might see his church during this special season. He invited her in to the decorated church with its manger. She asked, "Is this Christmas?" He answered, "Yes." She said, "It's beautiful." Then he took her downstairs, where parishioners were feeding about 175 homeless people. "Is this Christmas?" she asked again. "Well, uh, yes," he replied. She said, "It is very kind." Then they sat down for a moment, and she brought out from her bundles a little bag of oranges, offered them to him, and said, "This is Christmas, too." Simple gestures bring home the experience that underlies the story.

Anyone who gives a cup of water in Christ's name tells the story. Those nameless people who daily make their way to churches throughout the world to pray privately or to participate in liturgy, in much the same way that Morris Elfenbein and his old friends made their way to the synagogue each weekday, are telling the story. All the priests, religious, and laypeople who daily pray the liturgical hours alone or in groups, all those who daily pray the rosary—all are part of the great number of those who tell the story. Those who feed the hungry, who protest against injustice, who speak out against the immorality of modern warfare in the name of Jesus keep the story alive. Indeed, I venture to say that whenever our hearts reach out to embrace the sufferings of others, we are not only telling the story but also co-creating it with God. Telling the story, in other words, also enacts it.

The title of this meditation is "Who Will Tell the Story?" The answer that our reflections lead us to is "Everyone." At least, everyone is asked to contribute to the telling of the story. No one can, like Robbie Cox, tell the whole story, but we can all contribute our part to its full telling. Let's let the story live on our lips, "like starlings startled from a tree, / Exploding in a sky of revelation, / Deliberate and free."

## ❖ 15 ❖

# HOW IS THE CYCLE OF EVIL BROKEN?

> Therefore, just as sin came into the world through one man, and death came through sin, and so death spread to all because all have sinned.
>
> —Romans 5:12

At least since the time of Augustine, Christians have been accustomed to the idea that original sin and the tendency to sin have been passed down to each succeeding generation from Adam and Eve. But not many of us have thought much about how sin is passed on. Reflection on the human condition by social scientists may help us arrive at a deeper understanding of the history of sin and of grace inaugurated by Jesus.

Psychoanalysts have described a phenomenon called "repetition compulsion," defined by Ernest Jones in *Papers on Psycho-Analysis* as "the blind impulse to repeat earlier experiences and situations quite irrespective of any advantage that doing so might bring from a pleasure-pain point of view." For example, a woman who gets divorced from a demeaning and abusive man finds another who will treat her the same way. Moreover, the study of abusers of children regularly shows that they themselves were abused children. Over and over again, social scientists and therapists find that the sins of the fathers and mothers are indeed visited on their children. The evil or hurt that is done to one generation is passed on to the next.

In *Let This Mind Be in You*, Sebastian Moore acutely notes that human beings exist because God desires them into being. Hence, to exist at all, we are desirable, lovely, good, and the apple of God's eye. Yet most, if not all, human beings do not act as though they believe in their own goodness and worth. How do we get this way? Moore lays the blame at the feet of the conditional love we all receive in our families: "You're not a good boy if you don't eat all your spinach." "Where did we get such a bad girl? You can't be one of our family." "If you don't stop that, I won't love you anymore." A poor self-image leads to much unhappiness in life and to making many others unhappy as well. And the poor self-images of parents will have deleterious effects on their children as well.

Something similar occurs in social relations between groups. Children, for example, are not born with built-in racial, ethnic, or religious prejudice. They imbibe it with their mothers' milk, as it were, from a home and neighborhood environment poisoned by racial, ethnic, or religious slurs. Again we see that sinful attitudes and habits of thought and action are handed down from one generation to the next.

The same pattern can be discerned in the larger picture of social structures. The disparity between the nations of the Northern Hemisphere and those of the Southern in wealth and quality of life is based on a worldwide social system that favors the people of the northern nations over those of the South. Indeed, the system allows the North to exploit the South, often without either side being aware of the exploitation. With each passing generation, it seems, the poor of the Southern Hemisphere get poorer while their northern neighbors get richer. Moreover, most people in both hemispheres believe that the way things are is the way they are supposed to be. Nothing is expected to change.

In each of these examples, we can detect a sinful pattern that has a history. The cumulative effect of sins being passed down from generation to generation is overwhelming. Sin seems to roar down the centuries like a snowball that grows larger and larger as it rolls down a mountain. We can despair of ever stopping its deadly power. The darkness does seem to be overcoming the light. The nineteenth-century British poet Matthew Arnold summed up this feeling at the end of "Dover Beach":

> Ah, love, let us be true
> To one another! for the world, which seems

> To lie before us like a land of dreams,
> So various, so beautiful, so new,
> Hath really neither joy, nor love, nor light,
> Nor certitude, nor peace, nor help for pain;
> And we are here as on a darkling plain
> Swept with confused alarms of struggle and flight,
> Where ignorant armies clash by night.

Christians believe that "the light shines in the darkness, and the darkness did not overcome it" (John 1:5). The passage from Romans cited at the beginning of this meditation goes on to say: "But the free gift is not like the trespass. For if the many died through the one man's trespass, much more surely have the grace of God and the free gift in the grace of the one man, Jesus Christ, abounded for the many" (5:15). How does Jesus overcome the sinful pattern that seems so overpowering?

## FORGIVING AS JESUS FORGIVES

In two separate sessions of spiritual direction, a woman told me of an experience and an insight she had that may shed light on this question. She has given me permission to recount her experience.

The insight came as she was contemplating Jesus on the cross. She was behind the cross, as though looking down with Jesus on the scene in front of him. She realized that Jesus was absorbing all the hate and malice directed at him without passing it on. In other words, she saw that with Jesus the sinful pattern we have noted comes to a dead halt, because he does not allow it to make him a carrier. The woman also realized that anyone who really wanted to follow Jesus had to want to be like him as he accepted his passion and death. The pattern of sin is stopped when and insofar as people, by the grace of God, imitate Jesus in not becoming carriers of the contagion—when people do not allow the sins visited on them to control their attitudes and behavior toward others.

We need to make clear that Jesus does not absorb the punishment the way a masochist or a sad sack would. Jesus does not get covert pleasure from his suffering, nor does he turn the hatred aimed at him into self-hatred. He is not a victim who feels that he deserves what he gets. So, too, the Christian who follows Christ must not confuse masochism or the victim syndrome with suffering as Christ suffers.

But to suffer as Christ suffers is not an easy path, for Jesus or for us. A few weeks later, the woman was praying in a chapel and looked at a crucifix. In her imagination, she felt the horror of the Crucifixion, the horrible wrenching of Jesus' body and spirit as he hung there and received the hate and malice directed at him. At one point, she sensed that his face became contorted, almost demonic. She was frightened and asked God to be with her. Although she felt a peace come over her, she was still haunted by the image of Jesus dying so horribly. As she was telling me the story, I thought of Paul's saying that God "made him to be sin who knew no sin" (2 Corinthians 5:21). Could it be that it was a great struggle even for the Son of God to receive all this horror and hate without passing it on? Might not the woman's image of Jesus on the cross have reflected that struggle? After all, Jesus is also human, and it is no sin to have to struggle to remain loving and forgiving toward those who torment him. But he does bring it off, thus revealing the essence of who God is for us—namely, a self-sacrificing love that will not change no matter what we do.

If Jesus had to struggle to contain the effects of evil so that they would not spill over onto his tormentors, we who follow Jesus will know that same struggle. To forgive as Jesus forgives, to love as Jesus loves is no cheap grace. We all want our pound of flesh for wrongs done to us. Worse yet, as we have noted, we will, all unwittingly, tend to inflict on others what has been done to us. We need to allow into our consciousness the hurts and wrongs of our past life and ask God to help us forgive from the bottom of our hearts those who have inflicted them. Such healing of memories is a painful process, but it is necessary if we are to come to the wisdom Jesus expressed on the road to Emmaus: "Was it not necessary that the Messiah should suffer these things and then enter into his glory?" (Luke 24:26). Jesus would not be who he now is if his life had been different, if the Passion had not happened to him. Not that God wanted it this way, or that Jesus wanted it this way—to say that God wanted the Passion would be to say that God wanted these men to kill Jesus, wanted them to sin. But once done, it was necessary in order that Jesus be who he now is.

Another way to understand this "necessity" is indicated by the psychoanalyst Erik Erikson, who calls his final developmental stage the crisis between ego integrity and despair. Ego integrity, or wisdom, is "the acceptance of one's one and only life cycle as something that had to be and that, by necessity, permitted of no substitutions: it thus means a new, a different love of one's parents," Erikson explains in *Childhood and Society*. It would be despair if at the end of life we were so embittered that we wished we had been born to different parents, had a different upbringing, had lived a different life. But the wisdom Erikson speaks of and the new, different love of one's parents may require a very deep forgiveness of them and of the hurts inflicted by life. Such forgiveness is not an achievement of our wills, but a grace for which we beg in prayer.

We may be tempted to conclude that such wisdom is reserved for old age. It may be true that it is more likely later in life, but the following story illustrates that the grace can be available much earlier. In *Journey*, Robert and Suzanne Massie describe life with their son, Robert, who was born a hemophiliac. At nineteen, Robert Jr. was asked whether he wished that he had not had the illness.

This was his reply:

How can I—or anyone—wish that the most important thing that ever happened to me had not happened? It is like saying that I wish I had been born on another

planet, so different would I probably be. Put it this way:
I would not have it any other way. . . . Am I rational-
izing? . . . To say that would be to say that I have come
through the pain and troubles of my first eighteen
years with nothing to show for it. To believe that would
be to believe that I learned nothing of human nature
and kindness through all the years of hospitals, that
my parents were unable to impart more than an aver-
age sense of faith through all my setbacks. If this were
true, if having vanquished braces, bleeding, pain, self-
consciousness, boredom, and depression, I have not
added in any way to my appreciation of this life that
has been given me, then that indeed would be a mis-
fortune to be pitied.

The sins of the fathers and mothers are indeed passed on to
their children, in many different ways. But the history of sin is
not the only history we have. Even before the birth of Christ,
there was a history of grace, of the refusal to become a carrier
of evil, of the forgiveness of enemies, of the deep acceptance of
the hurts of life without passing them on. The mother of Jesus
herself, the sinless one, is a product of that history. But with
the death and resurrection of Jesus, that history has taken a
new turn, or dug more deeply into the marrow of human lives
and culture. In spite of the strength of the history of sin, which
seems to grow more implacable with the centuries, "there
lives," as Gerard Manley Hopkins says, "the dearest freshness

deep down things," the Spirit of Jesus, who makes it possible for wounded mortals like us to pass on care and love and thoughtfulness rather than fear, prejudice, hatred, and abuse. "Because the Holy Ghost over the bent / World broods with warm breast and with ah! bright wings."

# Epilogue

I hope that this book has helped you not only understand your own desire for God and resistance to its fulfillment but also engage more deeply with God. Books can only point the way toward such a relationship, note some potential detours and blind alleys, and, perhaps, give some insights. Of course, insights are a dime a dozen, and they don't do anyone any good unless they lead to judgment and action. Even if this book were a best seller (which would be a boon for my Jesuit province), it would not please me much unless I also knew that it had helped readers like you engage more deeply in a relationship of friendship with God. If you have been helped and are now looking for more guidance, you might want to check out my latest book, *A Friendship Like No Other*, also published by Loyola Press. But again I repeat: books are no substitute for actual engagement with God.

I have dedicated this book to my friends John and Denise Carmody. In John's final illness, he wrote a number of psalms, prayers to God that speak of his anger, his passion for justice, his love of his friends, and, most deeply, his love for God. It seems fitting to me to end this book with one of his last prayers. Perhaps you will find yourself praying to God with words like these.

You give us two commands
and let them merge into one.
We are to love you with all our heart
and to love our neighbors as ourselves.
More simply, we are to love always and everywhere:
our friends and our enemies,
the skies above and the earth under our feet.
For you are love,
and those who abide in love abide in you.
It could not be plainer, more sharply focused:
the greatest of your gifts is love;
love is our only crucial obligation.
I love you, God, and have for all my adult life.
I love you badly, distractedly, impurely,
but from the first I knew what your name meant,
first received the slightest inkling,
I knew you were all I needed or wanted
and my life gained purpose and order.
What shall I return to you
for all the favors that loving you has brought me?
I shall dwell in the thought of you,
the hope for you,
the trust in your care for me,
and the love that you pour forth in my heart
all the days of my life
and all your heaven to come.

# Annotated Bibliography

Barry, William A. *God and You: Prayer as a Personal Relationship.* New York: Paulist Press, 1987; *Paying Attention to God: Discernment in Prayer.* Notre Dame, IN: Ave Maria Press, 1990; *Finding God in All Things: A Companion to the Spiritual Exercises of St. Ignatius.* Notre Dame, IN: Ave Maria Press, 1991; *A Friendship Like No Other: Experiencing God's Amazing Embrace.* Chicago: Loyola Press, 2008. In each of these books, I develop ideas germane to the thoughts of this book.

Buechner, Frederick. *The Sacred Journey.* San Francisco: Harper & Row, 1982. This memoir aims to show how God has spoken in the ordinary events of the author's life.

Carmody, John Tully. *God Is No Illusion: Meditations on the End of Life.* Valley Forge, PA: Trinity Press International, 1997. Published posthumously by Denise Carmody, this book contains psalms and letters John wrote to friends during his final illness. It shows the sustained passion for God of a dying man.

De Waal, Esther. *Every Earthly Blessing: Celebrating a Spirituality of Creation.* Ann Arbor, MI: Servant Publications, 1992. Drawing on the Celtic tradition, the author presents prayers and blessings that reveal a deep faith in ordinary Celtic Catholics that God can be found in all things.

Hall, Thelma. *Too Deep for Words: Rediscovering Lectio Divina.* New York: Paulist Press, 1988. This practical little book to help people pray with Scripture includes five hundred Scripture texts.

Hillesum, Etty. *An Interrupted Life: The Diaries, 1941–1943, and Letters from Westerbork.* Translated by Arnold J. Pomerans. New York: Henry Holt, 1996. This is one of the finest testaments to the triumph of love over fear and hatred that I have read.

Moore, Sebastian. *Let This Mind Be in You: The Quest for Identity through Oedipus to Christ.* San Francisco: Harper & Row, 1985. Dense but brilliant, this work is by one of the most original spiritual theologians writing today.

————. *Jesus the Liberator of Desire.* New York: Crossroad, 1989. In the sequel to *Let This Mind Be in You*, Moore once again explores the meaning of the death and resurrection of Jesus for our lives.

O'Connor, Flannery. *The Habit of Being: Letters.* Edited by Sally Fitzgerald. New York: Farrar, Straus, Giroux, 1979. O'Connor's letters are insightful, poignant, spiritually and aesthetically wise, witty, down-to-earth, and, at times, enough to make you laugh out loud.

Williams, H. A. *True Resurrection.* New York: Holt, Rinehart, and Winston, 1972. The author maintains that unless the Resurrection is experienced in our real lives now, it is a dogma that has no relevance for us. He shows by examples from ordinary experience that we do experience resurrection now.